The Bent Guide
to
Gay & Lesbian
Amsterdam

Written by
Darren Reynoldson

www.pinkpoint.org

The Bent Guide to Gay & Lesbian Amsterdam
(Third Edition)
ISBN-13: 978-90-808851-2-7

Published by Pink Point
PO Box 16458
1001 RN Amsterdam

First published 2007

Book design and layout by: Matthew Curlewis - www.ludlowlounge.com
Front cover and back cover photographs: Bastiaan Aalbersberg
Front cover boys: Wolter ter Haar and Bart de Louwere
Back cover girls: Carolien Reijnen and Veerle Theunyssen

Illustrations used with kind permission of Ed Varekamp © 2007.
Homomonument illustration used with permission of Karin Daan.

Printed and bound by: Pantheon Drukkers

How do you define a homo-scene that's as historic and as mercurial as the change rooms backstage of a Cher concert (as well as similarly justifying and in turns denying rumours of its retirement)?

Well, we've scoured Amsterdam's queer underbelly (and boy, did it need a good scrubbing!) – from the blackest backrooms to the spotlights of so-bad-they're-good drag karaoke bars – to give you the most up-to-date and totally bent guide to everything that ain't straight about Amsterdam.

Yet even before the print dries on this, our surgically augmented third edition, Amsterdam will have lost another legendary venue, clubs will have changed names more often than Brangelina's adopted brood, or a drag queen will have broken a nail, had a hissy fit and gone into retirement.

So to ensure you get years of enjoyment from this, surely your most sensible purchase since *'101 Hilltop Hikes of Holland'* we strongly urge you to regularly visit our website: **www.pinkpoint.org** for each and every queer bending of Amsterdam's dynamic Gay and Lesbian scene.

A lot of gay guides get a lone reviewer to visit a city for a boozy week, just long enough to get the basic run down of the place to then write up a hazy first impression (mostly based on whether they got laid or not).

The Bent Guide to Amsterdam however, has been compiled by true Amsterdammers who are also volunteers at **Pink Point**: the world's first and *only* 7 days a week Gay and Lesbian information kiosk. Pink Point assists tourists (of any bent!), dispensing info on the world famous **Homomonument**, tips on one of the world's great gay capitals and directions to the Anne Frank Museum (just around the corner).

Assembled here is the culmination of close to a decade of advising visiting gays and lesbians where to go, what to do and generally how to get bent in Amsterdam. We go out dancing and boozing all year round and our success getting laid has nothing to do with whatever bitchy and highly subjective comments we have for a bar, club or queer venue. We're just naturally bitter and twisted. We blame the weather.

So - like any queer group and their local scene - we proudly admit passing judgement without fear of facts or favours. Accordingly, some reviews are little more than drive-by shootings off at the mouth, while others speak from more experience in smoke filled venues than the surgeon general would ever recommend.

As such, we've catalogued the city under the most basic of human urges:

We've tried to be as humourous as we are bitchy, as engaging as we are informative and (hopefully!) as entertaining as possible. You may also notice we try not to take ourselves too seriously, and hope you don't either.

Enjoy your stay and get bent!

GETTING YOUR BEARINGS

Found scattered throughout the confusing web of Amsterdam's alleys and canals we've compiled more than 300 gay and lesbian listings (not to mention more than a few not *entirely* straight ones best described as bent); creating a collection more diverse than a United Nations cocktail party, but with slightly less unity and cohesion. Not bad for a city of only 750,000!

Amsterdam - much like this book - is at turns sexy, hilarious, stunningly beautiful, outrageously confronting, cosmopolitan, small-bloody-minded and, because of the confusing layout, is best tackled one piece at a time:

The Vanilla Slice of town (p. 14) is centrally located on **Reguliersdwarsstraat**. Running parallel to the famous flower market this is where you'll find young twinks, yuppies and designer bars sprouting up all along the street.

The Camping Tradition along the **Amstel River** (p. 15) is home to traditional Dutch pubs, taverns and 'brown cafes.' Here you'll find small smokey old-style bars, and a somewhat camper (but very friendly) crowd who love a beer or ten and a good ol' sing-a-long.

The Dark Side of Amsterdam (p. 24) is centred along the infamous leathery belt of the **Warmoesstraat** containing sordid late night fetish bars, dungeon-like dark rooms, a plethora of porn vendors and, of course, more legendary 'coffeeshops' than you can poke a stick at, giggle uncontrollably over and then forget what the hell the joke was about in the first place.

The Pink Point of town is centred on the **Westermarkt** (p. 26). At the corner of the **Keizersgracht** and the **Raadhuisstraat** lies the **Homomonument**; the world's first monument commemorating historical persecution and contemporary celebration of homosexuality. Right next door is the world's first gay and lesbian information and souvenir kiosk - our very own Pink Point. And just around the corner is the COC - Holland's Gay & Lesbian Rights organisation.

The Back Side, centred around **Kerkstraat** (p. 35), is located across town not far from the tourist dominated **Leidseplein**. One of the oldest gay areas in Amsterdam, over the years it's diminished to only a handful of gay venues, mostly made up of hotels and porn shops, as well as the infamous Thermos saunas. Perhaps less dynamic than other areas, seasoned gay travelers will attest that our more relaxed backside can also be interesting to poke around in.

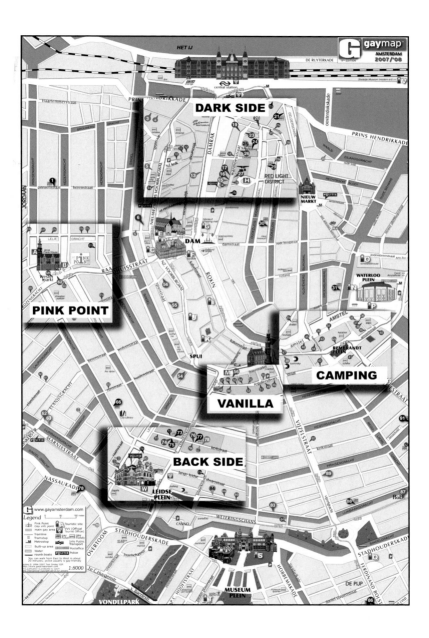

DRINK

Drinking is a way of life in Holland and Amsterdam's bars, clubs and brown cafes offer an incredibly diverse selection of venues: from sing-a-longs to sling-a-longs. But the one thing they have in common is a love of amassing piles of junk. Many Dutch bars (not just the gay and lesbian kind) are filled to their quaint wooden beamed ceilings with what looks like the remnants of a massive garage sale. But the most impressive collections are the differing 'types' that gather to drink and socialise in these junk yards with a liquor licence. No matter what you look like, no matter what you listen to, old or young, bulging or buff, there's a bar waiting to add you to its growing collection.

Most tourist's perception of Amsterdam is of a decadent, debauched 24 hour party city where *anything* goes. While the local attitude toward soft drugs, prostitution and homosexuality is one of legalisation and tolerance, the only thing that *really* goes in Amsterdam are the Euros from your pocket. A trading nation for centuries, the Dutch have made into a fine art worthy of any Rembrandt their masterful manner of extracting money from you.

Take beer, the social lubricant and one of Holland's chief exports (besides cheese, *'Big Brother'* and ecstasy). Amply demonstrating all that is Dutch Decadence, locals just *love* giving as much head as possible. Pull up a stool at any pub, brown café or nightclub and observe the quaint tradition of foaming up the glass as much as possible and then scraping off the suds above the rim with what a doctor uses when asking "Open wide". Here it means your pockets. Marvel at how the Dutch have convinced themselves that two fat finger's width of foam before one actually gets to the liquid amber is a good deal. You pay for a full glass but you only get to drink about 80%. But that's not all.

In Holland you don't actually buy beer, you rent it. When nature calls, expect it to call collect; you pay as beer enters *and* exits your system. Many venues - no matter how exorbitant the entry price - have some old troll lurking out the back ready to pounce for their pound of flesh should you need to spend a penny (or more precisely, up to 50 euro cents). And if you're caught short and need to relieve yourself in a dark street or simply into the canals (smelling as if designed for this very thing) expect a hefty fine if the Police catch you. You're better heading to the Warmoesstraat where some of the bars not only tolerate but also promote this very thing.

Sadly, the need to warm a bar stool before being invited to push another man's stool in has been severely challenged of late by an alarming increase in online ordering of home delivery rather than poking around for meat out in the markets. So, on a cold, wet mid-winter you might find more action warming up a modem than a martini.

But fear not, if you're the only one keeping the barman busy. The big brass bell hanging above the bar in most pubs and brown cafes is not in case of fire, stopping fights or for the inevitable playing of Abba's *'Ring Ring'*, but for buying everyone (and I mean EVERYONE) a round of drinks. In true Dutch style, even though these are mostly covered in more dust than Mariah Carey's *'Glitter'* DVD if you ring it, they will come.

Gay bars the world over may be pretty much the same - but not entirely in Amsterdam. Dark and smoke-filled they may be (hence: 'brown cafes'), but the traditional Dutch venues aren't so much gay bars (well, not as we know it, Jim) but more like public sitting rooms for a loose-knit queer family. So if you're after an authentic *Homo Hollandaise* experience check out the bars clustered predominantly along the **Amstel** river - as well as the trio along the **Zeedijk**. The crowds that gather here are mostly locals loyal to their specific bar and can vary wildly; from extremely young and camp to older straight white trash types. But mostly, this is where a LOT of regular guys (and more than a few girls) hang out to socialise, relax and brush up on their Eurovision song contest history.

Like any gay bar they can be a bit hit-and-miss and are somewhat daunting on arrival. Some, due to their intimate size, appear like you've gate-crashed a private party with *everyone* staring on your arrival, so much so it's often like walking into the local of the *'Village of the Damned'*. These are not bars that allow you to blend into the background and many a self-respecting gay man or lesbian may simply want to click their heels and wish there's no place like home. However, make like the Dutchies do, order a *Pils* (beer) or *Jenever* (cheap Dutch gin), swallow your pride and join in on a good ol' sing-a-long to some of the naffest music you'll ever hear this side of a Bucks Fizz reunion tour.

As a rule, the **Amstel Taveerne** is generally busiest with a somewhat older crowd early on, while the pretty young things bar hop from **Montmartre** to **Mix** before settling in late at **Entre Nous** or **Hot Spot**. Further up the Amstel, the ever more Anne Heche-like lesbian bar **You II** gets innundated with drunk Diesel Weasels mistakenly chatting up spunky lesbians after everything else has closed downriver. Lastly, nearby hustler bar **Music Box** may house a somewhat shadier crowd but the artful dodgers gathered here offer relief to more than just the other bars' dodgy music.

Amstel Taveerne

Map 42, p.15
Amstel 54
Daily from 5pm to 1am
Friday/Saturday till 3am
Happy Hour Mon to Thurs
7pm - 8pm
Who: *Mainly men; diverse, older (30s-40s) mixed Dutch crowd, some women & straights*
Wear: *Check Dad's closet*
What ♪: *Eurovision and Dutch drinking songs*
When's Best: *Early evening*

It's well worth a visit to one of Amsterdam's oldest, most popular pubs just to enjoy the genuinely welcoming atmosphere and soak up the hokey traditional setting of biersteins and dusty fake hams hanging from the wooden beamed ceiling. Simply pull up a stool at the bar and you're sure to have someone to talk to (most likely why the owners - to their eternal damnation - recently removed the huge tiled fireplace as focal point and replaced it with a hideous flatscreen for Eurovision karoke). Outdoor seating facing the Amstel river in summer.

De Barderij

Map 17 p.24
Zeedijk 14
Daily 3pm - 1am
Friday & Saturday noon
till 3am
Who: *Mixed Gay/Straight,*
older locals, few tourists
Wear: *Cardigans and*
corduroy
What ♪: *Varied*
When's Best: *Early*

Apart from the rainbow spirals outside the door you'd never guess this place is gay, but it's friendly and in a beautiful building that once was part of the old city wall. As well as traditional accordion sing-a-longs (!!!), it's also the den of choice for **Dikke Maatjes** (fuller-figured fellas) and also the **Netherbears** get together in its cave-like basement.

SPECIAL EVENTS:
Trad Dutch songs (& Accordian!) Thurs 8pm
Netherbears (downstairs) - see Bear Bars

De Engel van Amsterdam

Map 18, p.24
Zeedijk 21
Daily 1pm - 1am
Friday & Saturday till 3am
Who: *Proto-punks to shop-soiled skinheads*
Wear: *Casual butch drag*
What ♪: *Look at her!*
When's Best: *Sunny afternoons*

Ever pondered the philosophical question, How many angels can dance on the head of a pin? Well, this cute lil' *engel's* so tiny if there were any more than a handful of dancers here they'd be pinned to its delightfully historic tiled walls. As this newest addition completes a mini gay triangle with the **Queenshead** and **Barderij** along the always busy Zeedijk it's a great stop on a baby bar crawl - especially in summer when their perfectly placed sunny terrace by the canal gets packed for perving on passing trade. Oh, if in need of the surprisingly spacious toilets, watch out you don't get a bad head job before you reach the bottom of a stairwell tighter than a Botoxed butthole.

Entre Nous

Map 40, p.15
Halvemaansteeg 14
Sun to Thurs 8pm - 3am
Weekends till 4am
Who: *Mainly men – Women welcome*
Wear: *Casual*
What ♪: *Enough is enough!*
When's Best: *Late*

Why one bar (**Montmartre**) can be jam packed while another just across the narrow alley has only a handful of customers is one of Gay Amsterdam's great mysteries but offers one of its greater reliefs. The best thing going for Entre Nous is that it *isn't* Montmartre. Away from the noise, bustle and big gelled hair it's a quiet haven where one hit wonders of the 80s come to die (Flock of Seagulls, anyone?). Sadly, the considerably older and more sedate crowd makes it seem like some kind of waiting area for parents of the kids on too much cordial next door. However, after 3am, when other bars in the area close, this bar apparently buzzes (although, it's more likely the sound of a few old barflies debating the pop-perfection of Men Without Hats' 'Safety Dance').

Het Wapen van Londen

Map 44, p.15
Amstel 14
Daily 4pm - 1am Mon closed
Friday/Saturday till 2am
www.hetwapenvanlonden.nl
Who: *Older men & young Eastern European boys*
Wear: *Checks (of course!)*
What ♪ **:** *Oldies & 80s*
When's Best: *Late*

No longer need you fly to Prague to bounce a few Czechs! When Cor (former owner of hustler bar **Music Box**) married Josef (his Prague Prince) their resulting love-child is this cross between a cosy brown café and informal 'house of boys'. A compact bar attracting a clientele like the music on offer: a LOT of golden oldies with some 80s influences in the hair and fashions of the few East European boys on display. Sporting an odd mix of Czech flags and UK icons (the name means London Coat of Arms - as seen on the 1661 exterior), a rent boy's arrival can be about as reliable as a London double decker bus; you'll wait a while only to find 3 arriving at once (fares negotiable). Every 1st Saturday is Czech party. Outdoor seating facing Amstel river in summer.

Hot Spot

Map 33, p.15
Amstel 102
Monday 9pm - 3am
Tue to Thurs, Sun 4pm - 3am
Friday/Saturday till 4am
Who: *Mostly boys, women welcome & real men rarely seen*
Wear: *Casual*
What ♪ **:** *70s & 80s euro-trash*
When's Best: *Late Fri/Sat*

With more schoolboys here than a Neverland wine tasting event, you half expect this place to be shut down by a bunch of distraught nannies brandishing cups of cocoa and flannel blankets to stop the almost frighteningly younger crowd staying up *way* past their bedtimes. Personally, I'd rather show my Gran my Gaydar profile than hear Donna Summer's *'Hot Stuff'* ever again.

De Krokodil

Map 37, p.15
Amstelstraat 34
Daily 4pm - 2am
Who: *Mainly (older) men*
Wear: *Cardigans, pipes*
What ♪ **:** *Would you believe Kenny Rogers?*
When's Best: *Sunday arvos*

Another small, quiet and unassuming bar nestled between the ruins of the former iT nightclub and the Amstel river that is (perhaps too) easy to miss. Attracting an older crowd this 'croc' is the kind of place where even Paul Hogan would look like chicken. Gets busy Sunday afternoons (and assumedly on pension cheque day).

De Spaanse Ruiter

Map 6c, p.24
Nieuwezijds Voorburgwal 90
Daily 9am - 1am, Fri til 3am
Who: *Straight & a few Gays*
Wear: *Casual*
What ♪ **:** *Varied*
When's Best: *Sunday nights*

This small but cosy brown café run by a lesbian couple (Christa the daughter of the former owners & her partner Yvon) is so low key gay-wise even some of the staff have no idea why there's the occasional rainbow flag hanging outside. Still, with former bar staff from the **Amstel Taveerne** everyone enjoys a friendly welcome. Live music every Saturday. Also serves breakfasts for the early risers (or late nighters) as well as sandwiches & snacks throughout the day.

DE ENGEL
VAN AMSTERDAM

ZEEDIJK 21
zo. t/m do. 13:00 uur - 01:00 uur • vr. za. 13:00 uur - 03:00 uur
Tel: 020 - 4276381
de.engelvanamsterdam@orange.nl

Mix Café

Map 43, p.15
Amstel 50
Sun to Thurs 8pm – 3pm
Friday 6pm till 4am
Saturday 8pm till 4am
Who: *Mainly men – Women welcome*
Wear: *Casual*
What ♪: *Mod pop*
When's Best: *Late*

Some say that youth is wasted on the young but you can't help but smile when an entire bar is advertising space to Robbie Williams, merrily singing along to his radio hits (ok, with the exception of *Rudebox*). Accordingly, the kids behind the bar all seem to be frustrated rock DJs and are apparently not there to entertain you as much as themselves. But you're not tripping, don't be misunderstood and think she's Madonna, be a better man, let love be your energy and simply enjoy the good-natured feel. Hmmm, I think I've come undone and said something stupid.

Montmartre

Map 41, p.15
Halvemaansteeg 17
Sun to Thurs 5pm – 1am,
Friday/Saturday till 3am
Happy Hour 6pm – 8pm
Who: *Mainly 20s-30s men, some drag and a few real women (not all fag hags)*
Wear: *Anything as long as it sparkles, Honey*
What ♪: *Contemporary pop, 80's hits, traditional Dutch and (surprise!) Eurovision hits.*
When's Best: *up to midnight*

(see also: Drink – Drag)
While the 1880s French Bohemian *trompe l'oeil* tries to conjure up the Moulin Rouge, squeezed under an ever-changing ceiling (some window dresser's wet dream) the crowd is a millennium away, and is as firmly fixed in the 1980s as the overly-used gel in everyone's hair. Voted Best Gay Bar in Holland 7 times out of the last 10 years it amply demonstrates - like George W's re-election - why democracy is wasted on white trash. However, the often overly-packed, overly-young crowd are all very good-natured, out to have a good time despite (or even because of) the crush and can not only sing along to Whitney before the drugs, Madonna before the rug-rats & pre-chemo Kylie but can also re-enact ALL their old dance steps. Apparently the place to take one's straight girlfriends on a gay ol' time out, with all that big hair & shoulder pads jostling for supremacy the place can look a bit like a *'Dynasty'* cat fight, but it is friendly, fun and one of the few bars in the Amstel area consistently full.

Music Box

(see: Fuck – Hustler Bars)

't Leeuwtje

Map 45, p.15
Reguliersdwarsstraat 105
Daily 3pm - 1am,
Friday/Saturday till 3am
Who: *Old 'n newbies*
Wear: *Mouldy old jeans*
What ♪: *Golden oldies*
When's Best: *Early evening*

The newest addition to Amsterdam's gay strip is ironically, not only the oldest looking but probably the most over-looked (lying across the busy Vijzelstraat that divides the boys town from the hetro-ville that is Rembrandtplein). Since opening early 2007 it's done virtually nothing to draw attention to its new owner's sexuality apart from the rainbow flag outside. And that's its charm. No remodelling, no upmarket drinks or clientele, no techno - it's the gay bar time (and styling) forgot.

Prik

(see: Drink – Funky & Alternative)

The Queen's Head

Map 20, p.24
Zeedijk 20
Daily 4pm - 1am
Friday/Saturday till 3am
www.queenshead.nl
Who: *Mainly men; typical pub crowd leaning toward slightly older and skins (without Neo Nazi attitude). Women welcome*
Wear: *Fred Perry or Lonsdale gear, tatts and shaved heads*
What ♪**:** *Contemporary pop & Eurotrash.*
When's Best: *Late Fri/Sat*

The Queen's Head is a quaint old pub full of queer contradictions. While the front window is lined with a camp chorus line of Ken Dolls, inside it's most often lined with Skinheads & Sports-kit clad punters, chatting away amidst portraits of 50's matinee idols and more porno-graphically posed dolls in picture frames. The former owner - a bald, tattooed lad who dragged up once a week to become legendary Dutch Diva **Dusty** - retired the oversized pumps years ago but the queer mix of bra straps and braces has continued with a regular drag bingo show every Tuesday night. This is one gay bar that doesn't take itself too seriously and generally, has a friendly, unpretentious crowd that doesn't mind sharing a pint over a traditionally carpeted table.

SPECIAL EVENTS:
Tuesday Live Bingo/Drag

Rouge

Map 32, p.15
Amstel 60
Thurs to Mon 4pm - 1am
Friday/Saturday till 3am
www.caferouge.nl
Who: *Mainly (slightly older) men*
Wear: *Smart casual*
What ♪**:** *Every bloody Eurovision hit*
When's Best: *Late Fri/Sat*

Gay bars are so often filled with over-inflated macho poses, but here's a bar packed to the rafters with *real* old queens. Chintzy chandeliers, Art Deco lamps and (rather oddly, musical instruments stuck to the ceiling) high-light an impressive array of Dutch Royal Family portraits lining the walls. Queens, Princesses and other fairy-tale folk (autographed faded fag icons like Bea Arthur & Cher) watch from their cheap gilt frames while ever-so-slightly-past-their-prime punters (the types with cashmere sweat-ers still tied over their shoulders) sing along to yet another *Eurovision* (s)hit song reliving their nutbush city limits moves on the tiny dancefloor. But this cosy bar with fresh roses every week has a welcoming atmosphere as warm & fuzzy as the red velvet wallpaper and is so naff and so very *un-gay* as to be (almost) cutting edge cool (pity no-one's let the patrons in on the gag). The best bit, there's not a hint of irony to be found anywhere - including the own-er's all-singing drag alter-ego **Mandy More** (who seems to have snapped up retired Dutch Diva Dusty's dowdier hand-me-downs). Watch out for the dodgy door handle in the loos!

Spijker

(see: Drink – Leather, Bears & Skinheads)

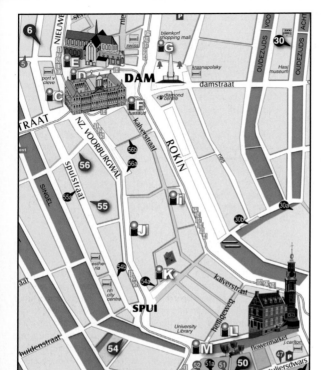

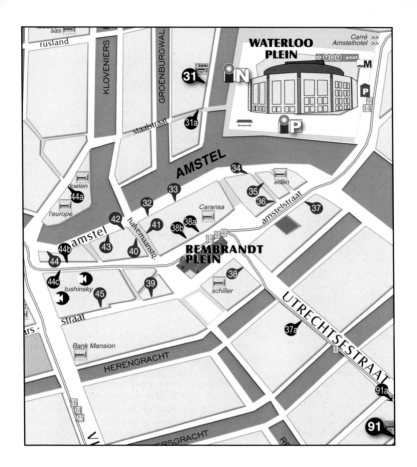

31	**Ebab**, *B&B*	40	**Entre Nous**, *bar*
32	**Rouge**, *bar*	41	**Montmartre**, *bar*
33	**Hot Spot**, *bar*	42	**Amstel Taveerne**, *bar*
34	**You II**, *women's danceclub*	43	**Mix**, *bar/café*
35	**Music Box**, *hustler bar*	44	**Wapen van London**, *bar*
36	**ViveLaVie**, *lesbian bar*	44a	**De Jaren,** *café/restaurant*
37	**Krokodil**, *bar*	44b	**Miranda**, *sex shop*
37a	**Kitsch**, *restaurant*	44c	**B1**, *sex cinema*
38	**Lellebel**, *drag bar*	45	**Café 't Leeuwtje**, *bar*
38a	**Escape**, *danceclub*	91	**ITC Hotel**
38b	**Studio 80**, *danceclub*	91a	**Backstage Boutique Coffeecorner**
39	**Reality**, *bar*		

Generally, the bars along **Reguliersdwarsstraat** (or Regular-Divorce-Street as it's more easily remembered) attract a younger 'preppy' crowd. Everyone sports the same *"I've-just-spent-hours-to-look-this-casual"* outfit and flit from bar to bar as the various happy hours tick by. So, you may suffer from a queer kind of *deja-vu* as you notice the same faces (and outfits!) almost everywhere you go. What's vital here is understanding where the locals - out to maximise their Euros - are at any given moment. The three major venues - **April**, **Soho** & **Exit** - share one owner and stagger their happy hours to ensure they don't compete for the same men like size queens at a Jeff Stryker lookalike competition. Early in the evening the **April's** happy hour packs them in like sardines (or pickled herrings, to be more properly Dutch). Later at midnight it's across the street at **Soho** (with various other 2 for 1 drink offers along the strip). Anyone left standing after 1am generally heads next door to **Exit** to dance off the booze or bump around their backroom.

Most of the venues here are large (well, for Amsterdam at least), modern and use pretty much the same formula found in bars from London to Sydney and Miami (overpriced drinks, cheesy music and locals awaiting the next plane load of fresh meat, er...tourists). However, a happy vibe ensures a reasonable crowd most nights of the week, especially in summer when the punters spill out onto the newly created 'terraces' (that's pavers with a white line painted on it to you and me). In winter however, outside the happy hours and weekend, the desolate strip can look more Gobi Desert than any gay ghetto.

April

Map 50, p.14
Reguliersdwarsstraat 37
Sun to Thurs 2pm - 1am
Friday/Saturday till 2am
Happy Hour 6pm - 7pm,
6pm - 8pm Sunday
www.cafeapril.eu

Who: *Mainly men; ditzy young things to sleazy old geezers. Women welcome*

Wear: *Jeans, T-shirts (artfully casual)*

What ♪: *Girly Pop Kylie, Madge, Britney bloody Spears*

When's Best: *Happy Hours*

The one thing the Dutch love more than a beer is keeping their wallets and purse strings firmly closed. Accordingly, this popular bar has even more of a crowd whenever there's a happy hour going on. The crush can be intimidating upon entering but make sure you push through to the back bar. Unlike other meat markets where you have to be constantly on the move working the room, this bar lets you strike the right pose while potential candidates are revealed by the turn of the slowly revolving floor. The various 2-for-1 deals on offer can lead to the place having a mad *quick-let's-get-shitfaced-while-it-lasts* feel that quickly descends into a *Pffwwaaaahh-you-look-awright-I-suppose-a-fuck's-outta-the-question?* that can be kinda fun depending on your mood. This can, however, prove problematic when trying to step off the revolving floor and you have no idea where the fuck the entrance is anymore… where your hotel is… what your name used to be… Hmmm, I don't remember eating *that*…

Arc

Map 46, p.14
Reguliersdwarsstraat 44
Daily 4pm - 1am
Friday/Saturday till 3am
www.bararc.com

Who: *Mixed/mainly men; early 20s to late 30s groovers & wannabes*

Wear: *Labels, Sweetie!*

What ♪: *One of those Chill-Out compilations that'll soon be heard on BBC gardening programs*

When's Best: *Cocktail hour*

(see also: Eat – Restaurants)

Despite opening in 2003 this 'designer' place (so very *Wallpaper** magazine circa 2001) is still considered a 'recent' upgrade to a scene so fixed in the city's legendary past some still can't quite work out why Freddy Mercury doesn't pop in for a pint anymore. Arc's open plan bar & restaurant is still kinda groovy, as are the people who artfully lounge on stylish sofas, eating stylish food and ordering Cosmopolitans (or whatever drinks the gals on *'Sex and the City'* used to down). You'll either love it or it'll leave you cold with its carefully studied neon cool, somewhat expensive prices & stick insect Fashion TV catwalks on the large video screens. While at times the only atmosphere seems to be whatever scent Calvin Klein is pushing, it's a good place to kick back in comfort (if you like looking good in a good looking setting filled with good looking people ignoring you but paying close attention to your labels). Oh, and the central reading table folds down at night into a dance floor (*very* Ikea-a-go-go!).

Exit Café

Map 48, p.14
Reguliersdwarsstraat 42
Wed, Thurs, Sun 11pm – 4am
Friday/Saturday till 5am
www.clubexit.eu

Who: *Mainly men; Women welcome*

Wear: *Casual & trendy*

What ♪: *Contemporary Pop - they even take requests!*

When's Best: *Early in week*

Directly under the **Exit** nightclub, this zinc and blue neon addition to the gay strip is so small, er… intimate you wonder why they bothered. Acting as chill-out room for the nightclub over the weekend, early in the week - when the nightclub upstairs is closed and only gay tourists, waiters and hairdressers crawl the strip - the 'Café' takes on those desperate punters after a beer and a bop on their tiny mirrored podium. Alas, lately it seems to be open about as often as Britney & K-Fed's wedding album.

Supperclub

(see: Eat – Restaurants)

Soho

Map 49, p.14
Reguliersdwarsstraat 36
Sun to Thurs 6pm - 2am
Friday/Saturday till 4am
www.pubsoho.nl

Who: *Mainly men; early 20's to late 30s, trendy, yuppie. Women welcome*

Wear: *Designer jeans & Ts*

What ♪: *Commercial House, some vocals.*

When's Best: *11 - 1am*

For 7 years this 2 storey *faux* English Pub has been a popular meeting spot for locals and tourists. The cosy fireplaces & Gentlemen's Club decore (studded leather armchairs, brass, gilt mirrors and art deco lamps) may look classy but the crowd is pure bangers-n-mash. Less National Geographic Society & more *'National Lampoon'* expect fewer intellectual discourses than beer-fuelled fumblings. Still, at least the pint prices aren't in Pounds Sterling. At times eerily quiet, at others packed to the rafters, it's busiest around Happy Hour (from midnight) then soon quietens down after 1am when drinks return to normal prices & the crowd stumbles on to **Exit** nextdoor or for a beer-soaking FEBO croquette.

If the vanilla slice of town is a little too Mark Hamill (circa *'Star Wars IV'*), those more drawn to the **Dark Side** are amply catered for along the narrow laneways fanning out from Centraal Station. While just another form of drag in many other cities, the Amsterdam leather scene is not to be taken lightly, so brush up on your hanky codes folks as there's more colours of the rainbow flagged here than Judy Garland would *ever* want to sing about. Perhaps a tad too serious, the belt of leather bars stretched along the **Warmoesstraat** can seem intimidating at first (but let's face it, if you can run the gauntlet of the hyper-hetero Red Light area wearing your chaps, you'll do just fine), and are in desperate need of upgrading what seem more like museum pieces to 70's homoerotica (who said it's only straight guys who need a *'Queer Eye'* makeover?). But, once inside any of the Amsterdam institutions that have remained virtually untouched for decades (some it seems containing more aspic than asspigs) you'll find the leather equivalent of *'The Stepford Wives'* with everyone standing around matching their sinister expressions to the same **RoB** or **Mr B** outfits in what appears to be the same dark and gloomy room with obligatory hanging rusty chains and yellowing posters of other leather bars around the world (apparently all called **The Eagle**). However, fear not if you're travelling light! Levis 501s and T-shirts aren't frowned on any more than everything else (leather's an attitude, not an accessory!) and even in the most hard-core venues it's not uncommon to hear Kylie or Madonna (remixed to buggery of course) or the swapping of cherry pie recipes - at least the one Crisco has on its can.

Amsterdam's leather boys also have a fairly fixed agenda for frequenting their bars: Early on it's the **Web** or **Cuckoo's Nest**; then **Argos** around 11pm; **Eagle** after 12 and then choosing between the **Cockring** for vertical dancing or **Dirty Dicks** for (you guessed it!) dancing of the dirtier variety. Bears and Skins (along with military and rubber lovers) are welcome and many venues host specific dress-up... er, fetish theme nights.

Argos

Map 27, p.24
Warmoesstraat 95
Sun to Thurs 10pm - 3am
Friday & Saturday till 4am
www.argosbar.com

Who: Men only; think Village People - without the camp glitterball aesthetic

Claiming to be the world's oldest leather bar (and by the looks of the faded, peeling posters on the walls of other long-gone leather bars around the world it may be right), this dark & narrow 3 level venue has long been the litmus test for discovering how Vanilla you *really* are. Apparently, little has changed over 50 years (alarmingly, the same may be said for more than a few patrons). While the imposing Brazilian owner Eduardo (rumoured to be the kind of guy Size Queens *love* to call "Sir") may not often be seen these days, you'll be watched over by an impressive bull's head hanging over the fireplace. Along with (surprise!) ominous chains and hooks hanging everywhere Argos resembles nothing more than a Tom of Finland inspired slaughterhouse; complete with fresh (and some past its use-by-date) meat hanging around in the slings and cubicles of the cellar darkroom.

(Cont.)

Argos
(cont.)

Wear: *Leather, uniforms or miltary (ok, 501s & Ts - no, NOT Calvin Klein!)*
What ♬: *Cruisy techno*
When's Best: *Later in the week between 11pm & 1am*

Cockring
Map 12, p.24
Warmoesstraat 96
Daily 11pm till 4am
Friday & Saturday till 5am
Entry: €3.50, Fri/Sat €5 (sometimes MUCH higher during tourist-milking events like Pride & Queen's Day)
www.clubcockring.com

Who: *Men only; diverse, masculine mid 20s to early 40s, gym, trim & slim*
Wear: *Jeans, tanktops or shirtless, trainers, some leather*
What ♬: *Hard techno downstairs dancefloor. Cruisy house in bar above.*
When's Best: *Fri/Sat after 12*

If you can stay for a drink or two without fainting from the at-times eye-watering videos on display you'll have butched it up with the best of the butch (and learnt what those large phallic poles lining the streets of Amsterdam are *really* for). This is a *serious* leather bar where the wearing of dead cattle is as required as the following code of conduct: NO smiling hello - a simple nod of the head is camp enough; NO squealing - unless it's like a stuck pig from *'Deliverance'*; and NO excessive waving of one's hands - unless it's to highlight that the pale band around your wrist is not a tan line from your watch but an example of the kind of ring Crisco can leave around a tub.

(see also: Dance – Regular)
Despite its historic notoriety and giant metal cockring hanging like some SM halo above the door, this place hasn't really been a leather venue since the Village People replaced their bikerman in 1995. But it can be just as cruisy as dead-cow boys from the leather bars next door often graze through. And just like the YMCA everything you need to enjoy is here as virtually every type of boy rubs shoulders (and other parts) in this extremely compact 3 level club. Often quiet during the week, after midnight Fridays and Saturdays downstairs gets filled real quick with shirtless muscle boys bathing in their reflections on the tiny mirrored dancefloor. Upstairs the dark & cruisy bar's video screens and private cabins provide enough motivation to bump and grind in other ways (although the coffin-like cabins' confined space could only really be enjoyed by necrophiliacs). Oh, and the big red button in the cupboards, er... sorry, cabins upstairs? Apparently if you and the occupant on the other side of the glass push it at the same time you get to remove all the romance and see the face behind the phallus. Finally, given the Ring's still infamous reputation, its *"live strip sex shows by international porn stars"* (Thurs, Sat & Sun) are *very* vanilla and are really more ads for Viagra's priapic power. And the occasional racier fucking, dildo & FF acts (usually on big holiday weekends) may cost somewhat more than your innocence as they overly-inflate the door price more than the boys on stage vacuum pump their pricks. While the boys behind the bar may not be able to suck their own cocks they're far sexier than any of the bored buff boys on stage beating their bloated boners to the beat.

SPECIAL EVENTS:
Nude Club Adam – 1st Sunday **(see: Fuck)**
Horsemen & Knights – 3rd Sunday **(see: Fuck)**
East/West Asian Disco – 3rd Sunday **(see: Drink/Ethnic)**
Sportswear – **(see: Fuck: Nude Club Adam)**

Cuckoo's Nest

Map 8, p.24
Nieuwezijds Kolk 6
Sun till Thurs 1pm – 1am
Fri/Sat 1pm – 2am
www.cuckoosnest.nl

Who: *Men only; diverse slightly older crowd (early 30s to mid 40s)*

Wear: *Jeans, leather, some suits (after work!)*

What ♪: *Varied*

When's Best: *Early*

Dirty Dicks

Map 15, p.24
Warmoesstraat 86
Fri/Sat 11pm – 4am

Who: *Men only; diverse slightly older crowd*

Wear: *Washable (on the hottest setting)*

What ♪: *Chilled Pop & Techno*

When's Best: *Early*

Eagle

Map 14, p.24
Warmoesstraat 90
Sun to Thurs 10pm – 4am
Fri/Sat 10pm – 5am

Who: *Men only; late 20s to over 40s, leather, skins, bears, rough trade*

Wear: *Jeans, leather, camouflage pants, track pants, uniforms & rubber*

What ♪: *Techno-style remixes of popular contemporary*

When's Best: *Late*

Virtually every bar in Amsterdam claims to be the oldest or first of their type but Cuckoo's Nest's claim to fame (apart from being able to sample someone else's lunch just after eating your own) is having Europe's largest darkroom. While the EU bureaucrats in Brussels are yet to tackle the thorny issue of standardising the height of slings throughout the continent, this expansive basement labyrinth certainly is one of the most interesting in town. An impressively cruisy maze of dungeons, nooks and crannies (handily a map can be downloaded from their website) can get surprisingly busy just after 5pm weekdays and during weekend shopping hours (*"Honey, I'm just popping into the hardware store to get nailed, er, nails."*)

Many a leather bar overly pushes the butch button or sleaze factor, but this one should win a truth in advertising award. Exceptionally dim lighting helps those not only unburdened by high standards in saying hello to darkened strangers but in hygene as well. Some may argue in its favour that it gets a good hosing down every month, while others will be wise not to ask about the liquid used (at least it smells like ammonia). Buzz the bell out front for entry if you're brave of heart and don't be disappointed if it seems you're the only one in the place. Fear not. Once your eyes adjust, order an obligatory drink, peer deep into the gloom and you'll soon notice a steady trickle of men emerging from the blackened bowels, giving the bar the weird feeling of being somehow connected to the lavs of Dr Who's Tardis (along with the odd lurking Master!)

SPECIAL EVENTS: Golden Shower evenings every last Thursday of the month. **(see: Fuck)**

This bar is yet another exponent of the famed *Amsterdamse* style Grandpa's-tin-shed-decorating-school. Need a tool to fix your bike? It's probably hanging from the ceiling of this darkly lit 3 level bar. Sharing many of the same punters from **Argos** across the street, it gets packed later with a (slightly) more diverse crowd (not just leather queens). A busy and cruisy darkroom downstairs stages monthly sling-a-longs for those evenings when you feel like taking it all in on your back (so it's probably wise to forget sampling the free popcorn at the bar as it's probably had more fingers in it than you'll *ever* manage). Ring the bell outside for entry and expect the oh-so-charming barman to chase you with a *very* bright torch if you head downstairs without first buying a drink.

SPECIAL EVENTS: FF Party 1st Sun/month **(see: Fuck)**
SOS every 2nd & last Sunday of the month **(see: Fuck)**

Furball

(see: Dance – Semi-regular)

Spijker

Map 74, p.35
Kerkstraat 4
Mon to Thurs 3pm - 1am
Fri/Sat 1pm till 3am
Sunday 1pm til 1am
Happy Hour 5pm - 7pm
www.spijkerbar.nl

Who: *Mainly men; diverse, slightly older crowd late 20s to early 40s. Women welcome.*

Wear: *Casual, jeans, Ts, some leather*

What ♫: *Trashy pop to cool techno*

When's Best: *Early*

Popular with locals and some passing trade this *'pool-porn-pinball'* bar doesn't quite fit its leather jacket anymore. Sure it's dark and down a few stairs but, although this 25 year old basement bar may have once been butch, even its eponymous giant nail (*spijker*) piercing the fireplace has been removed, leaving it as just another friendly neighbourhood gay bar still living in the 70s with a *serious* wood panelling addiction. Still, the décor at least compliments the pre-AIDS porn vids depicting guys with bad blow waves giving great blow jobs way back when everyone used to swallow and all the money shots were in slow motion (perversely, next to another TV showing cartoons with far better acting and more believable storylines). But, being the only bar of its kind this side of town it can get busy with a good crowd and a friendly relaxed atmosphere (especially from the sexy bar boys who flash a great smile for a good tip and pour the largest serves of *Jenever* this side of a Dutch retirement home). **Bingo** on Saturday nights, a welcome attitude towards women (unlike every other leather bar in town), a small but always busy pool table and the blackest upstairs darkroom you'll never see make this place a worthy visit.

Stablemaster

(see: Fuck – Jack Off Parties & Sleep – Gay Only Hotels)

The Web

Map 9, p.24
St. Jacobsstraat 6
Sun to Thurs 2pm - 1am
Fri/Sat to 3am

Who: *Men only; diverse slightly older crowd (early 30s to late 40s), Bears, Skins & Daddies*

Wear: *Jeans, leather, skin gear*

What ♫: *Techno/House*

When's Best: *Early*

Although at first glance the corrugated iron and rusting steel web of the exterior looks imposing, this early-opening bar is surprisingly friendly (especially in the large upstairs darkroom). The collection of cute little piggies tucked away in glass cases and lining shelves around the bar may make the place more *'Charlotte's Web'* than anything really sinister but upstairs sees it's fair share of swine-related activity.

SPECIAL EVENTS:
Wednesday nights at 10pm they hold a **lottery** (aren't all gay bars a gamble?) and on Sunday afternoons it can get quite busy when they serve **soup** or snacks at 5pm for those needy folk with a leather fetish to support.

Also stage occasional **Skinhead** special events (look out for flyers).

Leather Links

For a full, Holland-wide agenda of all Leather, Rubber and Fetish events, as well as info on **Playground** parties, ordering tickets, dress code rules, check out www.leatherpride.nl.

Also check out www.msamsterdam.nl for info on Motor Sportclub Amsterdam's regular leather and bike gear enthusiast get-togethers (and try not to smile at how many turn up on the tram in full gear!)

For monthly men-only SM parties check out www.avsh.nu

Bear Bars

Amsterdam has no fully dedicated Bear bar, but paw prints can regularly be found leading to:

Argos (see: Drink – Leather)
Café de Barderij (see: Drink – Traditional)
    Netherbears every 2nd & 4th Sunday in basement.
    Check www.netherbears.nl for full agenda
Dikke Maatjes
    Check www.dikkemaatjes.nl for full agenda
    (including their big bear bowling days)
Furball (see: Dance – Regular Events)
Prik (see: Drink – Funky & Alternative)
    Furball Café @ Prik every 3rd Sunday
Thermos Day Sauna (see: Fuck – Saunas)
    1st Saturday of the month 2pm - 10pm
The Web (see: Drink – Leather)

Skinhead Haunts

Amsterdam has no fully dedicated Skinhead bar, although the following bars often sport more Fred Perry gear than a Wimbledon sportswear shop:

Anco Bar (see: Sleep – Men Only Hotels)
Argos (see: Drink – Leather)
Eagle (see: Drink – Leather)
De Engel van Amsterdam (see: Drink - Traditional)
Queen's Head (see: Drink – Traditional)
The Web (see: Drink – Leather)

Amsterdam Gay Skins organise Skin events in Spring
    and Winter (see: Learn – Annual Events).
    Check www.agskins.nl for updated agenda.

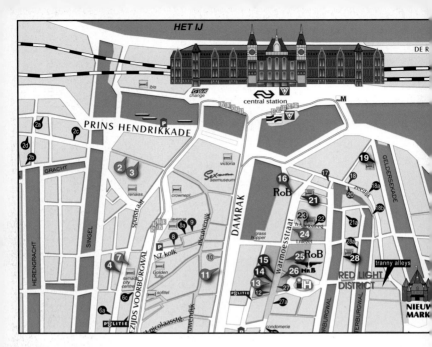

2	**Le Salon**, *sexshop*		15	**Dirty Dick's**, *leather bar*
2a	**Barangay B&B**		16	**Rob Accessories**, *leather shop*
2b	**Belhamel**, *restaurant*		17	**De Barderij**, *bar*
2c	**& K Centraal**, *shop*		18	**De Engel van Amsterdam**, *bar*
2d	**Stout**, *restaurant*		18a	**Little Thai Prince**, *restaurant*
3	**Alfa Blue**, *sexshop*		18b	**De Mask**, *fetish shop*
4	**Gays & Gadgets**, *shop*		19	**Black Tulip**, *leather hotel*
6a	**Female & Partners**, *women's sex shop*		20	**The Queen's Head**, *bar*
6c	**Spaanse Ruiter**, *café/bar*		21	**Stablemaster**, *J/O bar*
7	**4men**, *sexshop/cinema*		21a	**Paleis**, *v.d. weemoed*
7	**Boysclub 21**		22	**Centre Apartments Amsterdam**
8	**Cuckoo's Nest**, *leather bar*		23	**Boomerang**, *gay sauna*
8a	**Old Highlander**, *restaurant*		24	**Getto**, *bar/restaurant*
9	**The Web**, *leather bar*		25	**Rob**, *leather shop*
10	**Sauna Damrak**		26	**Mr B**, *leather shop*
11	**Drake's**, *sexshop/cinema*		27	**Argos**, *leather bar*
12	**Cockring**, *danceclub*		27a	**Winston Hotel**, *bar/hotel*
13	**Adonis**, *sexshop/cinema*		28	**Anco**, *leather hotel*
14	**The Eagle**, *leather bar*		28a	**Absolute Danny**, *women's sexshop*

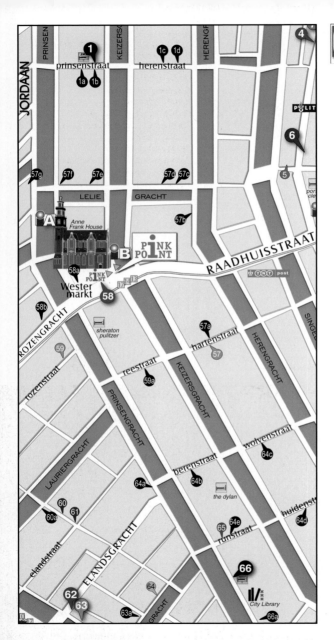

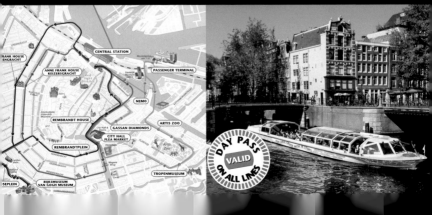

Muscle Marys, Twinks and Leather Queens can be found in virtually any gay-friendly city (and in many towns that are not). But to sample a more *underground* Amsterdam a visit to the various queer squats (empty buildings reclaimed by political activist communities), funky hangouts, alternative clubs and special one-off nights is a MUST for anyone wanting to avoid the usual *homo-robotica*, stamped-from-the-same-mould, Californian Porn-Star look that's taken over virtually every gay bar world-wide.

Best of all, in more than a few of the venues below you'll find Amsterdam's gay men and women actually hanging out together. How *very* Queer!

Blue Monday

@ Vrankrijk Map 55a, p.14
Spuistraat 216
Mondays only from 9pm
www.vrankrijk.org
Who: *Mixed; alternative queer men & women*
Wear: *Retro, leather, skins, goths, punks*
What ♪: *Hard Techno/Grunge*
When's Best: *Midnight*

Epicentre

Getto

Map 24, p.24
Warmoesstraat 51
Tues to Sun 4pm till 1am
Friday/Saturday till 2 am
Sunday from 4pm till midnight
www.getto.nl
Who: *Mixed; Lesbian, Gay and straight strays*
Wear: *Casual*
What ♪: *Chilled & funky*
When's Best: *Sunday cocktail party 5pm to Midnight.*

Other Side

Map 53, p.14
Reguliersdwarsstraat 6
Daily 11am - 1am
www.theotherside.nl
Who: *Pot Heads*
Wear: *Hemp shirts*
What ♪: *Trippy*
When's Best: *Any time*

The Queer night at the infamous and full-on **Vrankrijk** squat in the middle of town (look for the gigantic Lichtenstein-like Pop Art 'BOOM!' mural on the exterior) offers cheap beer and is a great place to smoke a joint or six. A real human zoo it makes Marilyn Manson look about as alternative as Laura Bush (although perhaps reminding the First Lady of her own hazy dealings in college?).

*NOTE: As we all know fur is murder, the only animal fashion accessory acceptable here is a big black dog at your feet.

(see: Dance)

(see also: Eat - Restaurants)
Tucked away amidst all the leather, porn and stoned tourist-filled coffeeshops along the **Warmoesstraat**, Getto's unassuming entry leads into a funky and very queer-friendly café, bar and restaurant out back. Retro décor and the cool staff make this a very friendly hang out, often with great DJ's, special events and tarot card readings (Sunday evening). Order a cocktail, chill out to the always cool music and let the buzzy queer atmosphere entertain you.

Not unlike Bill Clinton, if you *can* remember your trip to Amsterdam you couldn't have inhaled. The ONLY gay Coffeeshop in town (yeah, as in Dope, Dude!) doesn't serve alcohol but is, never-the-less, a great place to work up a gentle buzz before hitting the bars on this busy pink strip. Best to ignore your itinerary once you order from the 'special' menu. For more info on other Amsterdam coffee-shops visit: www.smokersguide.com.

Prik

Map 6, p.26
Spuistraat 109
Tues to Thur 4pm till 1am
Fri & Sat 4pm til 3am
Sunday 4pm till 1 am
(in summer from 12pm)
www.prikamsterdam.nl
Who: *Mostly men, late 20s to early 40s*
Wear: *Casual*
What ♪ **:** *Sparkling dance to fizzy pop*
When's Best: *Anytime*

Normally, the arrival of yet another prick on the Amsterdam gay scene wouldn't raise a pencilled eyebrow, but this Prick has been a MOST welcome additon to a town almost as accustomed to seeing venues disappear as the West Bank. For a change, Prik (meaning any drink with bubbles in Dutch) sparkles with fresh faces and ideas behind the bar (including being brave enough to have women serve the boys their beers), an ever-changing menu of nights (like Bingo & movie screenings), along with tasty snacks, a dizzying array of cocktails and even plenty of non-alcoholic drinks on offer. Queer or not, Prik is hot enough to attract a good mix of good-looking and good natured guys (and more than a few women) all comfortable enough in their sexuality for their drinking venue of choice not to have to look or behave like a gay bar, in an area that used to only see stray straights out crawling past the near-by red-light windows. More than the sum of its parts, it's not the décor or the bar itself but the friendly attitude of the punters and staff alike that gives this place its fizz. And their cute T-shirts - I ♥ Prik - make the perfect gay gift to take home.

Studio 80

(see: Dance)

Supperclub

(see: Dance)

De Trut

Not on Map
Bilderdijkstraat 157-159
Sundays only 11pm - 3am
Entry €1.50
Who: *Mixed; Gay/Lesbian, mostly young, funky alternative, University groovers*
Wear: *Loose & retro*
What ♪ **:** *Eclectic & Alternative (to put it politely!)*
When's Best: *Make sure you get there at least a half hour before the doors open as a line forms well before 11pm and they close doors when full.*

Despite *De Trut* ('old & frumpy' in Dutch) going for over 17 years, this basement queer collective is still one of Amsterdam's best kept and coolest secrets that happily demonstrates 'alternative' needn't mean suicidal Goths or angry young Punks. A non-profit concern and staffed on a volunteer basis (so be kind as their only payment is free beer!), all proceeds fund worthy gay & lesbian projects. It may all sound a little too politically correct but due to the exceptionally cheap entry & very reasonable drink prices the funky young things hanging here still know how to party like it's 1999 (probably 'coz most were in High School then & *still* don't have jobs to go to Monday morning). However, this ain't no metrosexual mosh pit folks, with a strict gay and lesbian door policy (although without having to give head at the door I'm not sure how it's ever policed). Still, it's nice to see Gen Xers reinforcing the sexuality barriers we spent the last 3 decades trying to break down. Ignore the at times, VERY dodgy music (I swear, last time they played Barry Manilow's *'Copacabana'* three times!) and just enjoy the laid-back funky vibe.

RIVATE ACCOMMODATION SERVICE
AFE. REASONABLY PRICED.
IMPLY THE BEST.
300 ROOMS & APARTMENTS
BOUT 140 CITIES WORLDWIDE
N MORE THAN 60 COUNTRIES
ebab
enjoy bed & breakfast
QUALITY TESTED
FRIENDLY HOSTS
COMPETENT TEAM

For a place that exists on dry land purely on the strength of some mighty dikes, Amsterdam is certainly no Land of the Lesbians. Like cities the world over Amsterdam's Women's Scene suffers from paltry patronage (what, is it genetic to stay home nursing cats and cups of tea?). Pitifully for a Gay Capital, only a handful (literally 5) lesbian venues open nightly with a sprinkling of other Sapphic events held at a few venues around town.

Nevertheless, while Amsterdam has always been a VERY boysy town, and the sight of girls behind glass selling themselves like take-away croquettes can be unnerving to our more politically minded sisters, there is a small but dynamic women's scene out there. Your mission: to boldly go where no man has gone before!

Custom Café Sugar

Map 60, p.26
Hazenstraat 19
Sun/Mon/Thurs 6pm till 1am
Friday/Saturday till 3am
www.les-bi-friends.com
Who: *Mainly women*
Wear: *Casual*
What ♪**:** *Diverse*
When's Best: *Early evening*

The newest chick off the block to sweeten the souring of Amsterdam's Sapphic social scene is a bit of a loungey throw back to the hippie-chick era. Thick with patchouli oil, throw pillows and funky painted wooden chairs, it's all very whole-wheat- tye-dye-earth-mother sort of thing that attracts a somewhat younger crowd than big sister Saarein just around the corner but is just as friendly.

Flirtation

(see: Dance - Regular)

45+ Vrouwen AVP

@ Paleis van de Weemoed
Map 21a, p.24
Oudezijds Voorburgwal 15
Every 1st Sunday, 3pm till 7pm
Entry: €2
www.amsterdamsevrouwenplek.nl
Who: *Women over 45*
Wear: *Casual*
What ♪**:** *Various*

For over 8 years Amsterdam's Women's Place has created a comfortable and non-confronting space for the more mature lesbian to hang out, talk, laugh, dance and meet others just as covered in cat hair and camomile tea-stains as they are. Formally held at the now defunct COC complex they've temporarily moved to **Het Paleis van de Weemoed** in hope of moving back to the resurrected COC one day. Sadly, I wouldn't hold my breath sisters!

Garbo

(see: Dance - Regular)

Getto

Map 24, p.24
Warmoesstraat 51
Tues to Sun 4pm till 1am
Friday/Saturday till 2am
Sunday 4pm till midnight
www.getto.nl
Who: *Mixed*
Wear: *Casual*
What ♪**:** *Chilled & funky*
When's Best: *Cocktail hour*

(see also: Eat – Restaurants)
Those not needing confirmation of how unattractive men and their obsession with sex can be may consider the **Warmoesstraat** a street best to avoid. BUT tucked away in this seedy straight porn and leather queen street, Getto is a welcome oasis in an overly testosterone fuelled strip. Funky retro decor, often with DJ's, special events and tarot readings on Sunday nights.

InRealLife

@ Crea Café Map 30b, p.14
Grimburgwal
Every 3rd Sunday of the month,
4pm till 9pm
www.inreallife.nl
Who: *Women only*
Wear: *Casual*
What ♪**:** *Diverse*
When's Best: *Not summer!*

Now part of the University of Amsterdam's music campus this former STD clinic (don't worry, you can sit in safety on the loo seats!) once a month becomes a dance and meeting place for lesbian and bisexual women. Attracts a somewhat younger student-ish crowd out for a cheap beer, game of pool or the occasional special party. Cute canalside terrace. Closed July/August for summer vacations.

Saarein II

Map 61, p.26
Elandsstraat 119
Tues to Sun 12pm till 1am
Fri/Sat till 2am Closed Mon
www.saarein.nl
Lunch 12-4pm, Dinner from 5.30pm
Who: *Mainly women; all welcome*
Wear: *Casual*
What ♪**:** *Diverse*
When's Best: *Early evening*

Along this cool lane of galleries, bookshops and jewelry designers you'll find a great split-level bar that defies Dutch 'brown-café' tradition – it's filled with natural light! As such, it's perfect for that late afternoon beer or relaxed game of pool (also friendly staff and good value food!). Established in 1978 as Amsterdam's first 'women only' bar, since the delightful Dia took over 8 years ago, it now welcomes all - to such an extent it now calls itself a 'mixed gay café' (oh how the more serious sisterhood would spin in their graves!). Meals are ferried from the Italian place across the laneway but don't seem to attract much of a mark-up along the way and €1 beer Happy Hour (that goes on for 2), Friday night Bingo and free WIFI access can make your Euros stretch even further.

SPECIAL EVENTS:
Also holds Transgender café **N00dles** every 3rd Sunday

Sappho

Map 90, p.35
Vijzelstraat 103
Tues to Thurs: 11am - 1am
Fri/Sat: 11am - 3am
Sun: 6pm - 1am
www.sappho.nl
Who: *Mostly women; mixed during week, Women Only Fridays*
Wear: *Casual*
What ♪**:** *Varied (often live)*
When's Best: *Friday nights after 11pm*

For some years now this art/music/theatre/lunch/women's café has been trying to breathe some life (albeit at times a very smoke-filled breath it is!) into the rapidly mortifying Amsterdam women's scene with an impressive (and, at times overly ambitious) weekly lineup of music, performance, open mic nights for singer/songwriters (not all of them depressing Tracy Chapman clones) cabaret, and whatever else they can think of to draw in a dwindling crowd. And, from time to time, it seems the bar itself has needed some resuscitation with it threatening to fold more often than a chinese fan. Still, it seems to have settled into a lively venue for anyone & everyone during week night live performances while Friday nights they stage the biggest weekly women's-only nights this side of Lesbos.

Spellbound

(see: Dance)

Trut

(see: Dance)

ViveLaVie

Map 36, p.15
Amstelstraat 7
Open Noon till 1am
Fri/Sat till 3am
www.vivelavie.net

Who: *Mainly women; gay men welcome*

Wear: *Casual*

What ♫ : *Shakira, Heart & Dutch divas like Anouk & Ilse de Lange*

When's Best: *Weekends early evening*

Established 26 years ago by **Mieke Martelhoff** (who received a medal from the Queen for her services to women) and partner Rosemary this cosy lesbian café/bar just off Rembrandtplein also more than welcomes gay boys (and even the occasional queer-friendly straight!). Busy especially in the evenings and weekends when they put away the tables and chairs to make room for more people this tiny bar can get more packed with lesbians than the mosh pit at an Indigo Girls gig. Even though the music can be a little too loud for deep-and-meaningful conversation, there's a good amount of flirting and a friendly vibe goin' on.

Vrankrijk / Blue Monday

(see: Drink – Funky & Alternative)

You II

(See: Dance)

saarein 2
mixed gay cafe

Elandsstraat 119   Amsterdam   Holland
020-6234901   www.saarein.nl
(maandag gesloten)

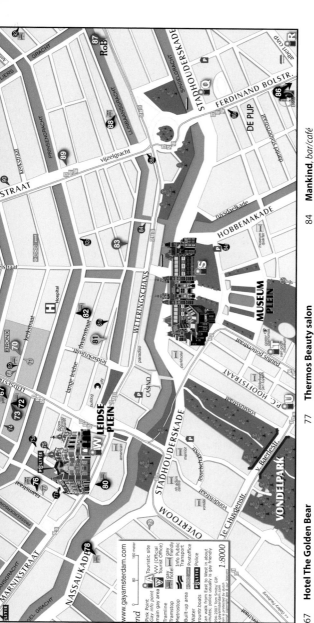

67 **Hotel The Golden Bear**
70 **The Bronx**, *sexshop/cinema*
71 **Thermos Night**, *sauna*
72 **Amistad Hotel & Apartments**
73 **Amistad Internet café**
74 **Spijker**, *bar*
75 **Habibi Ana**, *arabian bar*
75a **Gay Centre Spot B&B**
76 **Ebab B&B**
77 **Thermos Day**, *sauna*

77 **Thermos Beauty salon**
77a **Sugar Factory**, *night theatre*
78 **Hotel NL**
79 **HIV Foundation**
80 **Hotel Freeland**
81 **Cuts and Curls**, *hairdresser*
81a **JBK Gallery**
82 **Flatmates**
82a **Wenders**, *restaurant*
83 **Black Body**, *leather/rubber shop*

84 **Mankind**, *bar/café*
84a **Zuiderbad**, *swimming pool*
86 **Adriaen van Ostade**, *B&B*
86a **De Taart van m'n Tante**, *cake shop/ B&B*
87 **RoB**, *leather shop*
88 **Ebab B&B**
88a **Mail & Female**, *women's erotica shop*
89a **Pygma-Lion**, *restaurant*
90 **Sappho**, *lesbian bar*
92 **Radio Inn Hostel**

Gay scenes in virtually any Western city can be a little too white, middle-class and well, *homo*genous. Luckily, whitebread Amsterdam gets to dip itself in the cheesy gay melting pot that's been vastly enriched by the spicy addition of an *Allochtonen* flavour [although literally meaning "not of Dutch parents," it's come to be used by some as a politically-suspect term for Arabic, Moroccan and Turkish people]. While minority groups are well represented and welcome in all of Amsterdam's mainstream venues, the Arabic/Mediterranean, Black and Asian venues and parties are worth checking out for a non Dutch perspective to gay life in Holland [and where you'll be guaranteed NOT to hear either Kylie or any *Eurovision* song entrant – ok, maybe that delightful sheik-your-booty Turkish song that should've won in 2007!].

Arabian Dance (Nafar)

(see: Dance)

April

Map 50, p.14
Reguliersdwarsstraat 37

(see also: Drink – Trendy)
A sizable Asian crowd tends to regularly socialise here, happily tucked away under the oppressively low ceiling of the back bar (making the taller Dutch Rice Queens look like gay Gandalfs ducking into Hobbit's Chinatown).

Asian Dance

(see: Dance)

Habibi Ana

Map 75, p.35
Lange Leidsedwarsstraat 4/6
Sun to Thurs 7pm - 1am
Fri/Sat till 3am
Happy Hour 7pm - 9pm
www.habibiana.nl
Who: *Mainly men; younger Turks, Arabic and Moroccan guys (and their Dutch fans)*
Wear: *Jeans, T-shirts, some traditional gear*
What ♪**:** *Arabic flavas*
When's Best: *Friday nights*

While the Netherlands has gone through a turbulent time dealing with an influx of predominantly Islamic migrants, just off the beer halls of touristy **Leidseplein** is a slice of Turkish (and Moroccan and Egyptian) delight that displays Dutch integration and tolerance at its very best. Arabic for "my sweetheart" Habibi Ana is the self-proclaimed *"first and only Gay Arabic Bar in the world"* and entering is (kinda) like landing in a Middle East House Party (only without George W gate crashing it). In fact, keep an eye out for Ossama sightings – he's the surprise male belly dancer that sometimes performs on weekends. Sexy Turkish & Moroccan locals circle the tiny dance floor (OK, it's a Persian carpet) shaking their cute lil butts to traditional Arabic music, while onlookers clap in time and cheer.

Attracting other swarthy types (ie Mediterranean) as well as more than a few (somewhat older) Dutch guys there's a place on the comfy couches for everyone. There's even a Hookah (as in pipe smoking, not as in Red Light women), but alas, it's purely for decoration.

(Cont.)

Habibi Ana
(cont.)

In fact this cute lil' bar feels so good-natured and homey you expect the owner's mother to come by serving sweet pastries and rich dark coffee to all her son's new found friends, politely asking if the music can be turned down for the sake of the neighbours.

SPECIAL EVENTS:

Stichting Habibi Ana is a foundation providing support for *Allochtonen* (ethnic) Homo, Bi & Transgender men & women. Check out: www.stichtinghabibiana.nl

Lellebel
Map 38, p.15
Utrechtsestraat 4
Sunday 3pm – 3am
www.lellebel.nl

(see also: Drink – Drag)
Sunday night's camp carry-on has an 'Arabic flavour' with **'1001 Nights'** & DJ Said spinning the exotic grooves. Attracts in any case a lot of Mediterranean men, as well as rent boys from the nearby **Music Box**. Also hosts Indonesian nights. Look out for flyers or check website.

Reality
Map 39, p.15
Reguliersdwarsstraat 129
Sun to Thurs 8pm - 3am
Fri/Sat till 4am
Happy Hour 8:30 – 10pm
Who: *Mainly men; diverse Caribbean, Surinam & South American boys (and fans)*
Wear: *Casual*
What ♪: *Calypso-pop, salsa, merengue, reggae*
When's Best: *Weekends*

For nine years this small Calypso beach hut bar tucked away just off busy Rembrandtplein has been worth going to just for the sight of cute black guys from the former Dutch colonies showing local white folk how to *really* samba. However, if you're not out to dance, the level of the music may drive you away quicker than you can take the umbrella from your drink. Check website or gay press for various themed nights. www.realitybar.nl

Unlike more metrosexual cities such as London or New York - where new drag acts seek to continually evolve the art form - Amsterdam's drag *artistes* seem about as cutting edge as Benny Hill in a push-up bra. But, if you don't mind your drag unreconstructed and unabashedly old-fashioned, you can hear a show tune being mimed most nights at drag restaurant **'t Sluisje**, Tuesdays at **Queen's Head**, regularly at **Montemartre** and on occasion at **Exit**. But the reigning queens are to be found belting out beer songs nightly at **Lellebel**. There's also a 'dinner & show' venue **Paleis van de Weemoed** (www.paleis-van-de-weemoed.nl) in the Red Light District but it's mostly busloads of straight tourists out for a gay ol' knees up (and about as sophisticated as the frocks on offer are cheap). Otherwise local performance group **Chicks with Dicks** perform regularly (check out www.chickswithdicks.nl) and Coco Coquette puts on the hysterical Eurosong Travestival every year on the Sunday after the more traditional Eurovision.

The Dutch term for men who dress as women is *Travestie* and while it cruelly fits many a stumbling drunk Drag Queen (who's larger-than-life figures would never be confused with the real thing, no matter how many Heinekens you've downed!) the small Transgender community unfortunately, also tends to get lumped into this camp category. Their get togethers are often held in gay drag bars – such as **Lellebel**, & even lesbian bar **Saarein II** – which only adds to the gender confusion. The only dedicated Transgender venues are a once a month night at **Café de Gijs** and the 'erotic café' **Sameplace**, with women's SM group **Wildside** being very happy to slap around M2F and F2M members as well as those in 'transition' who identify as women. Even Arabic gay bar **Habibi Ana** has set up a foundation to support Transgender *Allochtonen* (Arabic ethnic minorities). Further info on support and self-help groups (for M2F, F2M and even parents of 'gender re-asssignment' children) can be found at www.wgtrans.nl or at the local Trans-portal www.travestie.org.

As for checking into your Hotel as one gender and stepping out later that night as another (and looking MUCH more fabulous) the **City Hotel** (www.city-hotel.nl) is only a handbag's throw from **Lellebel** and **Hotel Acacia** (www.hotelacacia.nl) is only a short stilleto'd stroll from **Café de Gijs**. Both are known to be more than friendly with whatever wigs, frocks and large sized heels you care to wear about the place.

In the Red Light district, trannies and she-males can be found in **Bloedstraat** and the other small lanes connecting the Nieuwmarkt to the Oudezijds Achterburgwal canal. (See Map p.24 - Tranny Alleys).

Lastly, every 2 years in mid-May the **Dutch Transgender Film Festival** is worth checking out and late August you can be a real Queen for a day on **Hartjesdag** (see: Learn – Annual Events) – the annual Amsterdam knees up of frocking up as the opposite sex (girls get to wear suits and ties – gee, yipee!).

Café de Gijs

Not on Map
Lindengracht 249
1st Wed of the month
Café open 4pm - 1am
www.t-en-t.nl

Who: *Transgender & Trans*

Wear: *Whatever makes you feel like the real you*

What ♪: *Varied*

When's Best: *After 8pm*

Owner and host Gijs isn't especially spiritual but feels it's his 'calling' to provide a safe and welcoming environment that respects all. So every first Wednesday of the month he opens the doors of his quaint lil brown café to Amsterdam's Transgender folk to socialise over a drink with other like-minded people.

A handy change room upstairs is provided for less brave souls not wanting to showcase their latest outfit on the tram getting there.

Drag Queen Olympics

29th April (Queens Day Eve)
Homomonument
7pm till midnight

Billed as the world's premier sporting event for drag queens (and surely destined for inclusion in the 2012 London Olympics if their oh-so-tasteful logo is anything to go by), this hilarious hairy knees up hosted by Pink Point's heart-of-gold-cum-media-whore **Jennifer Hopelezz** has become enormously popular with both straights and the local queer community flocking up to see the frocking up. With make-up facilities available (and more importantly free shame-reducing booze) to participants feel free to try your hand at a handbag fling, high heel sprint or tug of war (while marvelling at how hissy fit throwing never made the agenda). Check YouTube.com for clips of previous antics.

Transgender Film Festival

(see also: Learn – Annual Events)

Hartjesdag

(see: Learn – Annual Events)

Lellebel

Map 38, p.15
Utrechtsestraat 4
Mon to Thurs 9pm – 3am
Friday/Saturday 8pm till 4am
Sunday from 3pm till 3 am
www.lellebel.nl

Who: *Drag queens, Transsexuals and assorted fans (& boas, & tacky shoes)*

Wear: *"You can never have enough hats, shoes or gloves"*

What ♪: *Camp cabaret & Sssstunning show tunes*

When's Best: *Friday & Saturday nights*

Since 1997 host and owner **Desiree dello Stiletto** has been pouring drinks as well as her heart out during impromptu performances in this cute but tiny bar. Unlike a lot of drag where just badly mouthing the words to some tired old show tune is considered 'entertainment,' this delightful throw-back to camp cabaret actually displays (in between beer pulls) the vocal talents of its ladies, as well as their proficiency in O.T.T. hair and make-up. And if you thought Iraq's elections perilous to take part in, try sharing the spotlight with a Tranny waiting to terrorise a tune at Tuesday's Karaoke and Friday's Open Podium nights. Truly, these are evenings where even the blind can be shell-shocked by a local drag's stun and awe act.

SPECIAL EVENTS:

Mon - Whatever you want song requests
Tue – Global Karaoke (belt one out in Balkanese!)
Wed – Transgender Café
Thur – Red Hot Salsa night
Fri & Sat – Showtime (get a free drink for your drag act!)
Sun night – Carousel & Middle East/Oriental music

Montmartre

Map 41, p.15
Halvemaansteeg 17
Sun to Thurs 5pm – 1am,
Friday/Saturday till 3am
Happy Hour 6pm – 8pm

(see also: Drink – Traditional)
This venue regularly pulls in glitzy drag queens and other camp creatures who battle it out to be noticed in amongst all the chintzy decor and garish fittings.

Queen's Head

Map 20, p.24
Zeedijk 20
www.queenshead.nl
Who: *Skinheads, stray tourists & regular punters*
Wear: *Casual, sportwear & Fred Perry gear*
What ♪ **:** *Contemporary hits & camp classics*
When's Best: *Tuesday's Bingo*

(see also: Drink - Traditional)
For years Queen's Head used to be an Amsterdam drag institution due to the overwhelming presence of owner & host Diva Dusty (often seen weeding out undesirables by banging her sizable stilettos on unruly patron's heads until they got the point they weren't welcome!). After breaking up with her long-term partner and putting the wigs & frocks into mothballs (can you say "mid-life crisis" kiddies?) the new owners - while continuing the drag theme with a buxum Bingo night Tuesdays - haven't quite lived up to Dusty's oh-so-larger-than-life legacy. Still, the costumes are appropriately FAB, the gay banter good (albeit mostly in Dutch) and their sometime 'surprise guests' display the vast (!!?) wealth of local gay talent on Dutch TV (made up mostly - surprise surprise! - of former *Eurovision* singers).

N00dles

@ Saarein 2 Map 61, p.26
Elandsstraat 119
Every 3rd Sunday
www.n00dles.nl
Who: *Mixed; men, women & especially everyone in between*
Wear: *Cross dressing*
What ♪ **:** *Diverse*
When's Best: *After 5pm*

In December 2001, on the last day of the first ever **Transgender Film Festival**, a number of disenfranchised transgender folk decided to stop feeling so isolated and get out and do something - thus NOOdles was born. Ironically, their get-togethers are held in what used to be a strictly womyn's only bar, but now all genders and sexualities are made welcome, enjoying good food and good company. They also research & disperse information relating to Transgender issues as well as organising the parties that kick off the bi-annual **Transgender Film Festival**.

Sameplace

(see: Fuck – Weekly)

't Sluisje

Map 5, p.14
Torensteeg 1
+31 20 624 0813
Opens at 6pm
Shows Thurs to Sun
Reservations preferred
www.sluisje.nl
Who: *Drag queen afficianados with a taste for sequins & chips*
Wear: *Nothing you put on will compete Honey!*
What ♪: *Cabaret with cutlery accompaniment*
When's Best: *Showtime: Thursday to Sunday*

(see also: Eat – Restaurants)

What's the collective noun for a group of men in frocks? A sequins of Drag Queens. And this cosy (ie: small) restaurant is where you'll find them lining up to dish out drag performances like their wholesome, simple meals; kind of ordinary but with large serves of gusto. The tiny landing at the bottom of the stairs leading to the Ladies lav provides the 'stage' for a sequence of halfway decent mime numbers. The 'stars' do their best working the room (ironically, most-often filled with giggling straight gals on 'Hen's nights') but their performances never stray far from standard lip-synching fare that makes Danny La Rue look daring. While tributes to local Dutch Divas give a unique local flavour don't expect *'Priscilla, Queen of the Desert'* style production numbers as the poor girls would fall off their entrée-plate sized podium into someone's steak and *frites*.

Those of us who like a good sausage now and again will just love Dutch cooking! Mostly, *Nederlandse* cuisine involves boiling vegetables until there's no flavour left, mashing the fuck out of them until there's no texture and then placing a great big salty, fatty worst on top. Mmmmmm. It's simple, it's stodgy, but in the cold, wet winter months, man does it taste good (and warms you for those long bike rides home!).

Surprisingly, given the Dutch conquest of most of the Spice Islands centuries ago, too many restaurants have yet to work out what to do with chilli, lemongrass or basil. But, as always, there's a number of gay men and women training the local tongues to be a tad more daring than simply sampling the sad-looking croquettes from out of some fetid FEBO window.

Cafés and Lunchrooms

Backstage Boutique Coffeecorner

Map 91a, p.15
Utrechtsedwarsstraat 67
+31 20 622 3638
Mon till Sat 10am-5.30pm
Who: *Mixed Hetero & Homo*
What 🍽**:** *Coffee and snacks*
How much: *Good value*

Run by Gary - the last remaining half of legendary US cabaret duo the 'Christmas twins' - this wacky little café serves huge cups of coffee along with hand-made knitwear (of all things!) that line almost every surface as if some abandoned Grannie's knitting basket had been exploded by an over-zealous anti-terrorist squad. But the numerous crocheted holes decorating the place give an insight into not only the business plan of this quaint shambles of a café but possibly also the mind of the delightful owner who will launch into impromptu horoscope readings, confidently predict your future or brazenly point out your issues and then completely forget you're even there the next time he appears from his kitchen with your "foam in Rome" (cappucino).

Dolores

Map 56a, p.14
Nieuwezijds Voorburgwal
(opposite 289)
+31 20 620 3302
Open Sun to Wed 11am-7pm
Thur till 10pm, Fri/Sat til 3am
Who: *Mixed Hetero & Homo*
What 🍽**:** *Organic goodies*
How much: *Good value*

We've no idea of her sexuality but what gay boy could resist saying *"meet me at Dolores?"* And besides, with all their food & snacks being organic there's a reason for lesbians to hang out there too! This oh-so-cute lil' converted 106 year old tram shed (handily just opposite the postage stamp markets) is about as big inside as a stamp, but luckily has extensive outdoor seating in the summer months. The best place for a late night veggie burger or delicious crabcakes, Dolores is so good she recently scored a 9/10 from Amsterdam's bitchiest food critic (no, not me!).

Downtown

Map 51, p.14
Reguliersdwarsstraat 31
+31 20 622 9958
Daily 11am till 8pm
www.coffeeshopdowntown.nl
Who: *Mainly men*
What 🍽**:** *Sandwiches and light snacks*
How much: *Cheap & (mostly) cheerful*

Historically, one of the first gay cafes in Amsterdam, for some queer reason this tiny but always busy lunchroom is still *the* place for gay locals and tourists to muscle in and check out each other's lunch (on and under the table). The outside 'terrace' (complete with lifesize statue of a sleeping naked man) in the adjacent laneway leading to the flower market is (weather permitting) a nice place to people watch while passing the time it takes the microscopic kitchen to churn out a coffee, toasted sandwich or simple Asian noodles.

Hartenkaas

Map 59a, p.26
Reestraat 19
+31 20 626 5271
Who: *Lunchgoers*
What 🍽**:** *Sandwiches & deli goods*
How much: *Good value*

Hygiene freaks many of us are, the mere mention of 'gay cheese' may put the more squeamish off their *worst*, but tucked away in the *9 straatjes* (9 little streets) is a deli/sandwich bar that has the most impressive array of lunches this side of a Chi Chi La Rue porn flick. Hartenkaas (literally combining 'Heart' & 'Cheese') also has a wide selection of sandwiches, baguettes & other tasty deli items on offer, all lovingly prepared by a big cuddly bear type who, when asked why he flies a rainbow flag outside, replied with true Dutch matter-of-factness: *"Because I'm Gay."*

De Jaren

Map 44a, p.15
Nieuwe Doelenstraat 20
+31 20 625 5771
Open Sun to Thur 10am– 1am
Friday/Saturday till 2am
www.café-de-jaren.nl
Who: *Mixed Hetero & Homo*
What 🍽: *Simple rolls, cakes &*
good coffee in the day, modern
bistro at night
How much: *Reasonable*
prices in café, more expensive
in restaurant above

Although not a gay venue, no trip to Amsterdam should miss this big bustling 'grand central café' overlooking the Amstel river that gets its fair share of gay men and women. It's not that cheap, can be as noisy as a train station and the staff - cute as some of them are - are far too overworked to even notice you flirting. But if it's sunny push a granny into the canal to secure a spot out on the terrace facing the river. The perfect place to take in the wonderful scenery of cute canal houses, boats and bridges while imagining how much better it could be if the hideous Opera House/Town Hall across the water burnt to the ground.

Le Monde

Not on Map
Rembrantplein 6
+31 20 626 9922
Open breakfast, lunch & dinner
Who: *Mostly Hetero tourists*
What 🍽: *"Dutch food with a*
Brazilian smile"
How much: *Reasonable*

This busy Brazillian-style café seems pretty much like all the other white trash tourist-filled cafes clustered around bustling Rembrantplein. And, it is. Don't let the rainbow flags or ads in gay rags fool you. Apart from a few discretely placed gay maps and mags (and the odd bemused same-sex couple), there's little 'Mardi Gras' on offer. But the waiters are friendly enough and the serves reasonable. Few cruising opportunities unless you enjoy a *real* challenge.

Mankind

Map 84, p.35
Weteringstraat 60
+31 20 638 4755
Mon to Sat Noon till 10pm,
kitchen closes 8pm
www.mankind.nl
Who: *Mixed; mostly straight*
tourists from nearby museums
What 🍽: *Toasted sandwiches,*
cakes and light meals
How much: *Good value*

When it opened 17 years ago Frank & Jon's cute trad Dutch café/bar may have been the place for gay boys to meet, but now - despite prominently displayed rainbow flags outside and triangle motif on the coffee cups - this place mostly attracts unaware tourists needing a place to rest their feet after wandering through the nearby Rijksmuseum, art galleries and diamond shops. A narrow outdoor terrace overlooking the Lijnbaansgracht canal offers a relaxing spot in summer (although mostly in shade). Serves simple but good value meals and light snacks, but the kitchen closes at 8pm.

(No Name)

Map 64c, p.26
Wolvenstraat 23
+31 20 320 0843
Mon to Thurs 9am-1am
Friday/Saturday 9am till 3 am
Sun 10am-1am
Who: *Mixed Hetero/Homo*
What 🍽: *Asian noodles &*
fiiled sandwiches
How much: *Good value*

Unlike New York, this place is so good they didn't name it at all! A LOT of local lunchrooms think toasted sandwiches *haute cuisine* but this funky place serves great noodles (with real Asian flavours even!), decent breakfasts (unlike those sad fried eggs on white bread *uitsmijters* everywhere else) and is a cool place to hang, read a few mags & chill into the wee hours. Oh, the grey haired manager is *very* easy on the eye - pity the same can't always be said about their rotating art displays!

Stout

(see: Restaurants)

Pompadour

Map 64d, p.26
Huidenstraat 12
+31 20 623 9554
www.patisseriepompadour.com
Mon to Fri: 9am-6pm
Sat: 9am - 5pm
Who: *Mixed*
What 🍽: *Chocolates, cakes & pastries with a 'feel for drama'*
How much: *Not cheap but worth it!*

Cute as it is, Amsterdam in Winter can get pretty depressing as the cold grey of the streets merges seamlessly with a slate-coloured sky. The antidote? Just step into this cute lil chocolaterie, patisserie & tea room run by local gay boys Bram & Escu and take a BIG sniff of all those rich aromas. Or, for a real uplifting buzz, sample some of Holland's finest cakes, pastries and chocolate bon bons that'd bring a smile even to Donald Rumsfeld's sour puss. Also has a Tea House at Kerkstraat 148.

Small World

Not on Map
Binnen Oranjestraat 14
+31 20 420 2774
Tue to Sat 10.30 am till 8 pm
Sunday noon till 8pm
Who: *Mixed Hetero & Homo*
What 🍽: *Gourmet sandwiches & dishes from around the world*
How much: *Great value*

Yet another gay Aussie boy making good in Amsterdam (and apparently employing most of the Antipodean Ex-Pat community!). Showing the locals how a real gourmet sandwich is made, they recently were awarded the best *broodje* in town by Amsterdam's toughest critic (still not me!). They also churn out from their rather cramped corner store fantastic cakes and other exotic goodies from around our small world (and their lemon pie is to die for!). Also does great party catering.

Spanjer & van Twist

Map 57f, p.26
Leliegracht 60
+31 20 639 0109
Daily 10am till 1am
Friday/Saturday till 3 am
Lunch 10am till 4pm,
Sat & Sun till 5pm
Who: *Mostly Hetero*
What 🍽: *Contemporary café style*
How much: *Reasonable*

Not gay, but it's just around the corner from Pink Point and we like it, especially as it overlooks one of the tiniest & cutest canals in Amsterdam (often with a tone-deaf dwarf and out-of-tune guitarist busking from the other side on Summer evenings). A cosy 2 level café/restaurant with good food and service means the place is always pretty busy, and if the sun's shining you definitely want to grab a spot on their terrace overlooking the water. No reservations.

ZinK

(see: Health - het Marnix)

De Taart van m'n Tante (My Auntie's Cake)

Map 86a, p.35
Ferdinand Bolstraat 10
+31 20 776 4600
Daily 10am - 6pm
www.detaart.com
Who: *Mixed (Weight-Watchers don't-wannabes)*
What 🍽: *Faaaaabulous cakes*
How much: *Reasonable*

(see also: Sleep – Cake Under My Pillow B&B)
Just around the corner from the Heineken Brewery and Museum is an experience just as bad for those watching their waistlines. This *haute patisserie* tea house is so camp and kitsch it's like Dame Edna Everage bought Barbie's bakery then passed Pee Wee Herman the piping bag. The creators of these over the top wedding, birthday and who-needs-a-reason cakes don't know the meaning of restraint, producing architectural wonders out of marzipan and sponge cake. Especially full on weekends when normally reserved Dutch folk crowd around retro furniture, salivating & wide-eyed like kiddies on too much red cordial, getting stuck into sugar-coated-fetish-by the slice. Oh, light meals like quiches and muffins are also served but why waste time waiting for dessert? Bespoke (made to measure) cake orders by appointment.

Upstairs Pancake House

Not on map
Grimburgwal 2
+31 20 626 5603
Daily Noon till 6.30pm,
Saturday/Sunday till 5pm
Who: *Mostly tourists*
What 🍽: *Pancakes, pancakes & pancakes*
How much: *Good value*

Up one of Amsterdam's steepest staircases, into one of the smallest places (it seats no more than a dozen), with the lowest ceiling (tall boys beware of the dangling teapots!) you'll find some of the best pancakes in town, served by Amsterdam's most mercurial waiter. A sweet old thing on good hair days you do NOT want to be trapped in this tiny place when this old queen's not amused!

Wil Graanstra Frites

Map 58a, p.26
Westermarkt
Tues to Sat 11:30am - 6pm
Who: *Potato lovers*
What 🍽: *Dutch frites (fries/ hot chips)*
How much: *Cheap as...well, chips!*

What better way to enjoy Dutch cuisine at it's finest than a big paper cone of steaming hot *frites* smothered under a mountain of mayonnaise? Cheerfully supplying hot chips to chilled passers-by for almost 50 years, it's almost impossible to resist the wonderful aroma of fat frying wafting across the **Westermarkt** (good thing this family-run chip stand isn't any older, as it may have tempted one-time neighbour Anne Frank prematurely out of hiding!). Not gay (despite the rainbow flag), but the owners display a keen camp sensibility with send-ups of famous masterpieces decorating the exterior walls. Michaelangelo's 'God Passing Adam a Bag of Chips' & Van Gogh's 'Potato Eaters' are a hoot!

ARC

Map 46, p.14
Reguliersdwarsstraat 44
+31 20 689 7070
Lunch: Noon till 4:30pm
Dinner: 6pm till 10pm
www.bararc.com
Who: *Mixed; metrosexuals*
What 🍴**:** *Modern international*
How much: *Moderately expensive*

(see also: Drink – Trendy)

Decent modern menu, well presented if not a tad pretentious and over-priced. You pay for the ambience (very stylish & groovy) but the service (good eye candy that it can be) can, at times be a long time coming. Still, as groovy as they are they still know how to put together a half decent burger.

Bar 5

Map 1a, p.26
Prinsenstraat 10
+31 20 428 2455
Tues to Sat, kitchen open from 6pm till 10pm
www.restaurant5.nl
Who: *Mixed Hetero/Homo*
What 🍴**:** *Mod international*
How much: *Moderate*

Trendy split level bar/café in a cute laneway of the Jordaan area. Offers 5 cold and 5 warm lunch items such as club sandwiches, Nicoise salad or pastas and for dinner a five course 'surprise' menu of the chef's selection for the day. Luckily, they don't play the boy band of the same name.

De Belhamel

Map 2b, p.24
Brouwersgracht 60
+31 20 622 1095
www.belhamel.nl
Who: *Mixed Hetero/Homo*
What 🍴**:** *Mod international*
How much: *Moderate*

Situated on the canal recently voted Amsterdam's most beautiful to live on and facing straight down the (almost as beautiful) Herengracht, Belhamel is one of the most picturesque and romantic restaurants in all of Amsterdam. On a summer's night it's the perfect place to sit outside, enjoy the always good French/Italian-inspired Dutch dishes and simply watch Amsterdam float on by. But it's the authentic split-level Art Nouveau interior that will really make you want to take out your camera. Try not to sit upstairs above the always furnace-like kitchen on warmer nights, fret too much over the more than relaxed service, and make sure you enter by the beautiful bar from Binnen Wieringerstraat. Reservations vital.

Christophe

Map 57e, p.26
Leliegracht 46
+31 20 625 0807
Tues to Sat 6.30pm till 10.30pm
www.restaurantchristophe.nl
Who: *Mixed Hetero/Homo*
What 🍴**:** *French/Dutch*
How much: *If you have to ask...*

Earning a Michelin star is a big deal in a small town like Amsterdam, but losing one can cause SUCH a scene! Some local food snobs have never quite forgiven Chef **Christophe Roger** but thankfully, now that fashion has passed over fussy and overly-sauced french food, getting a table at this still excellent and extremely classy restaurant is no longer such a drama. Anti-cholesterol pills highly recommended.

11 (Elf)

Not on Map
Oosterdokskade 3-5
+31 20 625 5999
Daily Lunch Mon to Fri
Dinner 7 nights a week
www.ilove11.nl

Who: Mixed Hetero/Homo

What ⦿: *Think Jamie Oliver's restaurant Fifteen only with less hype, much less pricey and without being prepared by someone who'll leave Big Issue fingerprints on your bavarois*

How much: *Reasonable*

The once derelict Post Office HQ that towers above Centraal Station & the IJ Harbour now temporarily houses the Stedelijk Museum of Modern Art and a host of interior designers and architects. Doomed to be torn down in a few years and replaced with a monstrous development of ubiquitous penthouses, multiplex cinemas and shopping complexes it's become the centre of everything cool about edgy Dutch design. And perched at the very top – with an ever more encroached upon city view – is the very funky restaurant/bar/club 11. Like the rest of the building the expansive rooftop space hasn't so much been renovated as artfully gutted and minimally decorated with exposed rusting steel girders and two fantastically inventive (and cheap!) chandeliers made from old pot plant saucers.

Diners sit at long (and noisy!) communal tables (like some groovy inner city version of a *Witness* meal) flanked by screens projecting artfully shaky scenes of the city and surrounding dockyards when the spectacular sunset's done and the view just pin pricks of light. Next door another bare vaulted warehouse-like space gets taken over by performances, video installations or queer electronica and funky old skool club nights. Scheduled to finally close end of 2008 - what a shame!

Garlic Queen

Map 51a, p.14
Reguliersdwarsstraat
+31 20 422 6426
Wed to Sun 6pm – 1am
www.garlicqueen.nl

Who: *Mixed Hetero/Homo*

What ⦿: *Vampire's horror meal*

How much: *Reasonable*

None of the diners in this restaurant can be single or feeling lucky. A fantastically inventive menu extols the versatility of the odious bulb in every dish (they even have garlic icecream!), yet eating here could severly cut down on your social activities. This is a unique culinary experience to be enjoyed only with very close friends and loved ones, but (for the benefit of new found playmates) pack plenty of Colgate if your ring's feeling less than confident. Due to it's intimate size no bookings for groups over five people.

Getto

Map 24, p.24
Warmoesstraat 51
+31 20 421 5151
Tues to Thurs 4pm till 1am
Friday/Saturday 4pm till 2am
Sunday 4pm till midnight
Kitchen open 6pm till 11pm
www.getto.nl

Who: *Mixed Gay, Lesbian & some stray straights*

What ⦿: *Eclectic, spicy, home-style cooking*

How much: *Good value*

(see also: Drink – Funky & Alternative)
Filled mostly with queer diners on any given night, Leather Queens and Lipstick Lesbians hunker down happily cheek-by-jowl to graze on Getto's eclectic 'home cooking' style menu (expect kangaroo steaks, spicy curries or a wicked Getto BBQ Burger). Although good size serves of well prepared and fresh food translates into being busy most nights, their tiny downstairs kitchen (at times) struggles to feed everyone without reasonably long waits. Make sure you take good conversationalists along (or simply listen in on the nearby goss).

Harkema

Not on Map
Nes 67
+31 20 428 2222
Mon to Sun 11am to 1am
www.brasserieharkema.nl
Who: *Mixed straight/gay*
What ▮: *International*
How much: *Moderately expensive but good value*

Large, stylish and almost always buzzy (but bloody noisy!) brasserie in an old tabacco factory along this little known (to tourists) theatre-filled laneway leading off the Dam. Not necessarily a gay hangout or even (to our knowledge) gay run (although the candy-striped wall is VERY queer indeed) its good, well prepared and presented food, pleasant service and a trendy crowd makes the place worth a visit.

Hemelse Modder

Not on Map
Oude Waal 9
+31 20 624 3203
Tue to Sun from 6pm
www.hemelsemodder.nl
Who: *Mixed straight/gay*
What ▮: *International*
How much: *Moderately expensive*

The stark interior of this place kind of belies the rich history of a restaurant that seems to have been in Amsterdam forever. Formerly one of *the* queer dining venues, it now attracts a mostly 'mainstream' crowd due to consistently good quality food and wine on offer, but still pulls in a regular gay and lesbian clientele.

Hot Peper

Not on Map
Overtoom 301
+31 20 412 2954
www.depeper.org
First Sat of month from 7pm
Who: *Queer, alternative & transgender*
What ▮: *Organic*
How much: *Dirt cheap*

This squat café in the former Film Academy has an organic not-for-profit restaurant open 4 days a week, and turns queer the first Saturday of the month. On my last visit we were served fried gnocchi (not recommended) but for €6 for soup, main course, DJ's and shows, who can complain. Call to reserve.

Kitsch

Map 37a, p.15
Utrechtsestraat 42
+31 20 625 9251
Daily 6pm till late
www.restaurant-kitsch.nl
Who: *Mixed Hetero/Homo*
What ▮: *French-ish & International*
How much: *Moderately pricey*

From the welcoming Madonna (no, I mean the *real* virgin!) in the window to the playful menu (ever seen oysters & french fries called 'pussy & potatoes' before?) you know the owners of Kitsch have a keen camp aesthetic. But this brightly coloured, multi-level restaurant is serious about serving good food at reasonable prices. And best of all, unlike so many others, rather than having to eat early & then stand around an empty bar waiting for the boys to arrive, here the kitchen doesn't close until midnight.

Little Thai Prince

Map 18a, p.24
Zeedijk 33, +31 20 427 9645
Daily: *4pm - 10:30pm*
Who: *Mixed; straight/gay*
What 🍴: *Thai*
How much: *Good value*

Diagonally across the Zeedijk from **Queen's Head** local queens (and some passing straights) get treated like Princes with good value and tasty Thai dishes. Make sure you try host Gin's mouth watering *Tod Man Pla* fish cakes.

Moeders

Not on Map
Rozengracht 251
+31 20 626 7957
Daily 5pm - 11:30pm (ish)
www.moeders.com
Who: *Mixed Hetero/Homo*
What 🍴: *Traditional Dutch stodge*
How much: *Reasonable*

For all their modern morality the Dutch are a practical folk and nothing more accurately reflects their simple palate than Moeders ('mothers' in Dutch). For 15 years this quaint restaurant has dished out 'comfort food' like stews, mashes & worsts as hearty as the welcome by the waitresses is warm. But make sure you've no unresolved Mother issues as the gaze of hundreds of maternal eyes (guests can submit pics of their dear ol' Mums for display) may turn even the most well-adjusted child into a nervous Norman Bates fingering the mis-matched cutlery. Cute canal-side terrace May to October.

The Old Highlander

Map 8a, p.24
Sint Jacobsstraat 8
+31 20 420 8321
Daily Noon till 1am Closed Mon
Kitchen closes 10:30pm
Who: *Mixed Hetero/Homo (quite a few leather boys)*
What 🍴: *Hearty meals*
How much: *Good value*

Right next door to **The Web** (and sharing the same owner) this narrow restaurant and "Amsterdam's only Scottish bar" is a bizarre cross between *'Braveheart'* and *'Memoirs of a Geisha'*. A kooky mash up of oriental-themed bamboo bridges to pass o'er before you can tuck into their all-day Scottish breakfasts, it gets its fair share of leather boys pigging out on real Size Queen meals before pigging out as Size Queens next door. Get in early if you want to secure a table before heading next door for a beer.

Pygma-Lion

Map 89a, p.35
Nieuwe Spiegelstraat 5A
+31 20 420 7022
Tue to Sun 5:30pm -10pm
www.pygma-lion.com
Who: *Mixed Hetero/Homo*
What 🍴: *South African*
How much: *Moderately expensive*

Tired of run-of-the-mill food? Try food running off the Kalahari instead at this stylish design restaurant in the 'antique' quarter of Amsterdam. They specialise in traditional South African family recipes cooked with exotic ingredients such as crocodile, zebra and antelope - and offer a good range of vegetarian meals as well. The food is an amazing fusion of European, Asian and African tastes. Outside tables in the summer months.

Saturnino

Map 52, p.14
Reguliersdwarsstraat 5
+31 20 639 0102
Daily Noon til Midnight
Who: *Mixed Hetero/Homo*
What 🍴: *Italian*
How much: *Reasonable*

Not gay but this busy Italian place - at the start of the always popular Pink Strip - has been feeding us fagatinis for years with simple but hearty pastas and pizzas.

Stout

Map 2d, p.24
Haarlemmerstraat 73
+31 20 616 3664
www.restaurantstout.nl
Daily 10am til Midnight
Who: Mixed Hetero/Homo
What 🍽: International
How much: Reasonable

Catch the different moods at this lively spot on the bustling Haarlemmerstraat. Good coffee and fruit shakes early in the day, excellent salads and interesting sandwich lunches, followed by a dinner menu of fresh, intriguing combinations. The ten course taster menu for two is thoroughly recommended and very good value. Elbow your way onto the terrace or lounge cushions in sunny weather for some laidback people-watching over a glass of champagne.

't Sluisje

Map 5, p.26, Torensteeg 1
+31 20 624 0813
Opens at 6pm, Wed to Sun
(shows Thur till Sun)
www.sluisje.nl
Who: Mixed Hetero & Homo
What 🍽: Grilled meats, sausage, chips & salads
How much: €36 for 3 courses + €3.50 showcharge

(see also: Drink – Drag)
At this throwback to a horrifying 'theatre restaurant' expect nothing fancier or higher class than good sized serves of simple grilled food. After all, the Drag shows dished out here with gay abandon are the real main attraction. It's all good fun as diners sing along, while tucking in to hearty meals in between camp cabaret numbers. ***NOTE:** The *'Fee for payment of wigs and costumes'* notice at the bottom of the menu may make you choke on your chips when you realise you're contributing more to maintaining historic relics rather than updating anyone's wardrobe.

Supperclub

Map 56b, p.14
Jonge Roelensteeg 21
+31 20 344 6400
www.supperclub.nl

Restaurant:
Sun to Thurs 7:30pm – 1am
Fri/Sat 7:30pm – 3am

Lounge/Bar:
Sun to Thurs 7pm – 1am
Fri/Sat 7pm – 3am

Who: *Mixed Hetero & Homo*
What ⚭: *International fine dining (but eaten lying down & off your lap!)*
How much: *Fixed menu (approx €65 plus wine); expensive - but worth the experience.*

Weekend reservations at least 3 weeks in advance!

Supperclub is a super groovy, super cool, super expensive and super weird cross between a warehouse rave, slumber party and a *haute cuisine* restaurant. Downstairs the lounge/bar looks like it's from Kubrick's *'2001 A Space Odyssey'* – curvaceous, super slick & shiny. Upstairs, two giant all white double-decker beds flank the vaulted room leaving the floor vacant for performance art, DJs, dancing or whatever funky weird shit the lunatics running the place want to dish up. Leave all your table manners at home, slip off your shoes, stretch out on the soft, white mattresses, chill to the always cool music (check out their range of self-titled CDs), take a massage on offer and settle in for a loooooong but entertaining (and often disturbing) night.

The surprisingly good 5 course menu (which you have no choice in - alongside sometimes being served hors-d'oevres with forceps from a dog bowl) can take ages to appear, so make sure you go with company you *really* enjoy (and don't mind being slightly embarrassed in front of). On our most recent visit our wine waiter (clad head to toe in black vinyl, looking like the fetish love child of Darth Vader & Cat Woman) bent over in front of us so we could sip from his tubular tail the champagne contained in 2 huge rubber sacs hanging between his legs. This is not the kind of place you need to remember which fork to use first! The waiters (sometimes looking all Kate Moss junkie chic, at other times are ultra-glam transexuals) add to the über-theatrics by treating you with artful disdain - but can be quite friendly if you don't react badly to what can be shocking service. Lastly, the unisex toilets are marked Hetero & Homo. If you're bored it's fun just waiting outside watching straight suit & tie types fretting over whether they should relieve themselves in front of gay patrons or their female colleagues.

Walem

Not on Map
Keizersgracht 449
+31 20 625 3544
Open Daily 10am – 11:30pm
Who: *Mixed Hetero & Homo*
What 🍴**:** *Mostly Mediterranean*
How much: *Reasonable*

On a Summer's day no-one on this sunny terrace along the Keizersgracht pays any attention to renowned Dutch architecht Rietveld's artfully designed facade. They're all too busy either watching the passing parade along the always busy canal or they're eagerly awaiting a table. Of course, there's always a good number of gay boys checking out each other's lunches as well.

Wenders

Map 82a, p.35
Prinsengracht 598
+31 20 638 0899
Wed to Sun 5pm – Midnight
Kitchen closes 10:30pm
www.restaurantwenders.nl
Who: *Mixed Hetero & Homo*
What 🍴**:** *Traditional Dutch with French & Asian inspirations*
How much: *Reasonable*

Ah, memories, misty water-coloured memories... Years ago Chef Rene and head waiter Sjoerd put on a faaaaabulous wedding breakfast for Australia's first legally married gay couple (that's me and my man!) at their former café Ruiten beer. Now, with their own modern take on the Dutch 'brown café' (less clutter and much more light) they serve good honest food as well as spicing up traditional, local fare with cunning use of French & Asian influences - even decent vegetarian choices on offer. And all in a warm and friendly manner. Outdoor seating facing the delightful Prinsengracht canal in Summer.

One of the best things about wandering around the winding streets and narrow laneways of Amsterdam is stumbling across some great little shop, funky fashion outlet or one of the many fetish establishments the city is infamous for. Pay special attention to a slew of boutiques in the **Jordaan** and **Negen Straatjes** (9 little streets), the Flea Market on **Waterlooplein** and, for labels (sweetie!), **PC Hoofdstraat**. How shopping misses being included in the Gay Games amazes me as it's surely our most popular homo recreational sport (ok, *second* most popular!).

But what makes a particular store gay? A bitchy shop assistant gossiping on the phone rather than telling you your bum *does* look big in that? Openly gay store owners are scattered across town rather than clustered in any particular gay ghetto and some may display a rainbow flag, but there's plenty more that don't. So we've thrown in a handful just to get you started on your marathon of merchandise meandering.

[Whoever eats from the butcher won't get thinner]

& K Centraal

Map 2c, p.24
Haarlemmerstraat 8
+31 20 422 2708
Mon to Fri 10am – 7pm, Sat
10am – 6pm, Sun noon – 6pm

Original, simple, affordable, arty homewares - often their own & K label - in this home and gift shop on the Haarlemmerstraat, a great shopping street in the Jordaan. (OK in fact there aren't any antiques, but we ran out of room on the next page!).

JBK Gallery

Map 81a, p.35
Korte Leidsedwarsstraat 159
+31 20 624 9871
Open daily
www.jbkgallery.nu

A permanent exhibition of the unique 'extreme porcelain' artworks of Dutch ceramist Jeroen Bechtold. The gallery is open daily but not strictly regular hours as Jeroen is often at work on site and closes the door. A phone call before visiting is recommended.

Kusmi Kim

Map 57c, p.26
Leliegracht 4bg
+31 20 423 4430
Wed to Sat 11am till 6pm
Sunday Noon till 4pm,
www.kusmikim.com

Fine tea and fine art. Check out the gallery's paintings and delicate teapot collection while sipping fragrant steaming brews. How civilised, how very gay!

Springfield

Map 57g, p.26
Prinsengracht 122
+31 20 489 4285
rupertspringfield@hetnet.nl

Cute lil' antique shop across the canal from the Anne Frank House.

Truelove

Map 1b, p.26
Prinsenstraat 4
+31 20 320 2500
www.truelove.be

(see also: Sleep – Queer Friendly Hotels)
Great antique and curio shop with a Bed & Breakfast above.

Ed Varekamp

Map 57a, p.26
Hartenstraat 30
+31 20 625 7766
Viewings: Sat 1pm till 5pm

Although straight, renowned Amsterdam artist Ed Varekamp has a *very* queer imagination, producing a great collection of naive and (at times) *very* naughty and gay and lesbian (and hetero!) themed paintings (as featured throughout this book), as well as lithographs and wonderfully erotic glazed pottery. Open Saturday, by appointment, or try your luck & ring his bell!

Butler's

Map 64e, p.26
Runstraat 22
+31 20 676 4760
Mon to Fri: 11am - 7pm
Sat till 6pm
Sun: 2pm - 5pm

Having a Butler draw you a bath is a rare treat but top stylist Marcel offers fag-plush pampering with designer baths, showers & fittings to match the chic candles, oils, towels & robes on offer. Stocks Scapa Home, Gunther Lambert, Culti, Birkenstock, Boudoir, Bevora & Flou.

Dom

Map 54b, p.14
Spuistraat 281
+31 20 428 5544
Daily 11am - 8pm, Thur til 9pm,
Sun 1pm - 8pm
www.dom-ck.com

Ever wondered why window dressers seem to have never escaped the camp stereotyping? Blame Christian Koban - the man behind Dom. I'm not sure about his other stores in Cologne, Paris or New York but in Amsterdam this trendy (but at the same time oh so very cheap) furniture and home ware store is camper than a boy scout jamboree.

Frozen Fountain

Map 66a, p.26
Prinsengracht 629
+31 20 622 9375
Mon: 1pm - 6pm,
Tue to Fri: 10am - 6pm
Sat: 10am - 5pm
www.frozenfountain.nl

Less a furniture shop and more an interior design museum and art school showcase, this place is a must for anyone into cutting edge homewares, lighting, fabrics & furniture. Run by Dick Dankers & partner Cok de Rooy (now there's a Euro-porn duo name, if ever I heard one!) they exhibit as well as sell the best & innovative of all Holland's bright young things & established designer labels.

Gays & Gadgets

Map 4, p.24
Spuistraat 44
+31 20 330 1461
Mon to Sat: 11am - 8pm,
Sun: 12pm - 8pm
www.gaysandgadgets.com

G&G is the gay shopper's equivalent of the kid in a candy store metaphor: books, jewellery (for *every* part of your body), club and gym wear, lubes, party tickets and more gadgets than a queer agent on her Majesty's Secret Service could search for - that is, if lurid, kitsch, pink, fluffy or simply faaaabulous are key words. The perfect place to shop for that hard to find homo-wedding gift when you're not sure if you want to congratulate or bitch slap the happy couple!

Kitsch Kitchen

Map 58b, p.26
Rozengracht 8-12
+31 20 428 4969
Mon to Sat: 10am - 6pm
www.kitschkitchen.nl

Never let it be said there's no truth in advertising any more. This place is a riot of cheap Mexican kitsch, colour, camp, gawdiness and bright plastic glam for your kitchen (& other tacky household needs). Sunglasses recommended & leave your gay good taste behind!

Pink Point

Map 58. p.26
@ Westermarkt - Corner of
Keizersgracht & Raadhuisstraat
+31 20 428 1070
Daily 10am - 6pm
www.pinkpoint.org

(see also: Learn - Information Services)
The best selection of queer-themed T-shirts, postcards, fridge magnets, rainbow-coloured souvenirs and cute Delft Blue same-sex kissing couples in Holland. Not to mention the friendliest and most helpful service in town, free advice on gay & lesbian events around town and info (in 11 languages!) on the nearby **Homomonument**.

P**i**NK PO**i**NT

gay & lesbian information / souvenir kiosk

homomonument - westermarkt

open daily 10 - 6 pm (limited opening hours in winter)

www.pinkpoint.org

The ultimate gay shopping experience

GAYS & GADGETS

Spuistraat 44 • 1012 TV Amsterdam • Tel. 020 - 330 14 61

Open: Mon. - Sat. 11am - 8pm • Sun. 12noon - 8pm

www.gaysandgadgets.com

we provide you with complete, comprehensive and reliable gay tourist information.

American Book Center

Map 54a, p.14
Spuistraat 12
+31 20 625 5537
Mon to Sat: 10am - 8pm
Thurs til 9pm, Sun: 11am -
6:30pm. www.abc.nl

The English Bookshop

Map 60a, p.26
Lauriergracht 71
+31 20 626 42 30
Tue to Sat 11am - 6pm
www.englishbookshop.nl

Intermale

Map 55, p.14
Spuistraat 251
+31 20 625 0009
Mon: 11am - 6pm
Tues to Sat: 10am - 6pm
Thurs til 9pm Sun: Noon-5pm
www.intermale.nl

Starting out in 1972 with just U.S-sourced under the counter stick mags and a handful of cheap remainder books, ABC is now one of the largest English-language booksellers in Europe, and the first mainstream bookshop in town to establish an extensive gay and lesbian section (fiction, non fiction and some porn). 10% discount for students & teachers. Also hosts Treehouse seminars & writer's workshops.

A well-curated selection of books in this cosy bookshop on a peaceful, tree-lined canal in the Jordaan. No pressure, plenty of time to browse and a few comfy chairs for sampling before you buy. Also the venue for various writing workshops and readings in partnership with local, international writers. Check www.wordsinhere.com for schedule.

This low ceilinged sub-street level men's-only book shop feels like stepping back to a time when all gay bookshops had a somewhat underground feel. Certainly their extensive vintage porn collection out back reminds you of those furtive one-handed readings of youth (well, it does mine!). They also stock a good selection of travel guides, fiction, mags, cards and some videos. Large selection of English titles as well as Dutch, German, Spanish & French.

Vrolijk

Map 56, p.14
Paleisstraat 135
+31 20 623 5142
Mon: 11am – 6pm
Tue, Wed,Thurs
& Fri: 10am – 6pm,
Sat til 5pm
Sun: 1pm – 5pm
www.vrolijk.nu

Around the corner from the Royal Palace are the Kings and Queens of Queer-Lit. With Holland's largest selection of Gay & Lesbian fiction - boy's books line one wall and girl's the other (just like a heterosexual dance!) - as well as biographies, self-help books, travel guides, transgender and religious titles, erotica, comics, kids books, postcards, magnets, calendars and T-shirts. Don't forget to nosey upstairs in their extensive erotic and gay-themed DVD collection. Look out for regular Sunday readings and book signings.

Xantippe Unlimited

Map 64a, p.26
Prinsengracht 290
+31 20 623 5854
Mon 1pm – 7pm,
Tue to Fri 10am – 7pm,
Sat 10am – 6pm, Sun 12 – 5pm
www.xantippe.nl

Rightly, for a bookshop named after Socrates' wife, Xantippe has an extensive selection of specialist women's studies, lesbian literature and emerging women writers, as well as a wide range of general travel, art, fiction, cookery and kids books Socrates himself would be green with envy to own.

Absolute Danny

Map 28a, p.24
Oudezijds Achterburgwal 78
+31 20 421 0915
www.absolutedanny.com
Mon to Sat 11am – 9pm
Sunday 12am – 9pm

Unlike other sex shops this one's the kind of place you could gladly take your old Mum. (Ok, maybe after you've sat her down with a nice cup of tea and told her what you've *really* been doing with your life). Stylish, not at all sleazy and run by a woman who even designs some of the fetish gear herself.

The Big Shoe

Map 57d, p.26
Leliegracht 12
+31 20 622 6645
www.bigshoe.nl
Wed to Fri 10am – 6pm
Thursday till 9pm, Saturday
till 5pm

Not gay, and not especially fag-friendly if you're a big bloke prancing about their store in a pair of size 46 pumps, but just for its range of large shoes it deserves a mention. Also stocks real Men's shoes up to size 50.

Black Body

Map 83, p.35
Lijnbaansgracht 292
+31 20 626 2553
Mon to Friday 10am – 6:30pm
Sat 11am – 6pm
www.blackbody.nl

Nestled amongst the genteel antique shops and art galleries near the Rijksmuseum, this small shop is jam-packed with a great selection of contemporary art of it's own: rubber and leather wear as well as assorted fetish gear like cockrings and butt plugs. Not for the faint-hearted!

Condomerie

Not on Map
Warmoesstraat 141
+31 20 627 4174
Mon to Sat 11 am – 6pm
www.condomerie.com

Since it opened in 1987 the *"world's first specialised condom shop"* has broken through that gossamer-thin membrane of prejudice regarding the oldest known prophylactic and brought a sense of fun along with an all important safe sex message. With hundreds of different types of condoms, in an amazing array of sizes and styles, you're sure to discover one to make your nether-regions Netherlandic chic.

DeMask

Map 18b, p.24
Zeedijk 64
+31 20 620 5603
Daily 11am - 7pm,
Thurs till 9pm, Sunday till 5pm
www.demask.com

Love the feel of latex, the crack of the whip, or a stilleto heel in your face? This is the place for all the rubber, latex and leather gear (rubber bras and panties to heavy leather suspension body bags) a Domina and her slave could ever want. Shops also in New York, Barcelona, Nurnburg and Munich.

Female and Partners

Map 6a, p.24
Spuistraat 100
+31 20 6209152
Tue to Sat 11am - 6pm, Thurs
til 9pm, Sun - Mon 1pm - 6pm
www.femaleandpartners.nl

Mail & Female

Map 88a, p.35
Nieuwe Vijzelstraat 2
+31 20 623 3916
Daily 11am - 7pm
www.mailfemale.com

Mr B

Map 26, p.24
Warmoesstraat 89
+31 20 422 0003
Daily 10am - 6:30pm, Thurs til
9pm, Sat 11am - 6pm,
Sun 1pm - 6pm
www.misterb.com

RoB

Map 87, p.35 & Map 25, p.24
Weteringschans 253 (closes
autumn 2007)
Warmoesstraat 71 (opens
autumn 2007),
Warmoesstraat 32
+31 20 428 3000
Mon to Sat 11am - 7pm,
Warmoesstraat shops open
Sundays
www.rob.eu

Robin and Rik

Map 65, p.26
Runstraat 30
+31 20 627 8924
Mon 2pm - 6.30pm,
Tue to Sat 11am - 6.30pm

It's always interesting how many Amsterdam venues or businesses claim to be the first or largest of their kind. And sometimes, that means a cheeky game of shady semantics. Take Female and Partners and **Mail & Female** (below) for example. Since '92 "Amsterdam's first erotic store for women" has stocked great lingerie, sex toys and party clothing in a relaxed, non-sleazy sex shop.

Meanwhile, Mail & Female claim to be "Europe's first and best loved shop by women". But, truth be told, running a 'mail order service' in erotic articles by and for women for the past 10 years isn't quite the same as selling off the street. However, with a new "offline" store they can now legitimately claim to be more physically open than a Sharon Stone interrogation scene.

This world-famous leather shop in the Red Light District is a supermarket of sex toys and fetish gear (and is great fun just standing outside watching straight tourists gape open-mouthed at their always eye-watering window displays of beer barrel sized butt plugs and donkey kong sized dildos). Rotating exhibitions of gay/fetish art line the walls, friendly service (often a little too attentive when buying items of a more 'intimate nature'), impressive range of leather, rubber and military wear, sex toys, accessories and also a tattoo and piercing salon upstairs. What more could a bad gay boy want? Also in Berlin.

For over 30 years RoB's has been the place for all your leather, rubber and twisted gear. This Dark Side Emporium has expanded its Empire to stores in Paris, London, Brussels, Zurich, Manchester and Berlin and - finally! - moved its flagship store closer to the Amsterdam leather action of the Warmoesstraat to provide the passing bug-eyed tourists more sinister shocks than an Iraqi jail cell.

For more than twenty years Robin & Rik have been hand-making made-to-measure leather pants, jackets, chaps and vests, as well as a range of caps, belts and wristbands, all from their atelier in the quaint Negen Straatjes (9 little streets) area.

The Shirt Shop
Map 46a, p.14
Reguliersdwarsstraat 64
+31 20 423 2088

Stylish and trendy shirts, tank tops and knitted pullovers down the other end of Reguliersdwarsstraat. Open 7 days a week!

Stout
Map 64b, p.26
Berenstraat 9
+31 20 620 1676
www.stoutinternational.com

In English 'stout' may conjure up visions of big buxom gals, but in Dutch it means 'daring' or 'naughty'. So be a big brave girl and dare to try on some of Amsterdam's naughtiest lingerie & erotic jewellery.

Stravers
Not on Map
Overtoom 127
+31 20 616 9973
www.stravers-shoes.com

As Stravers stocks women's shoes up to a whopping size 47 (that's 31cm!) and fits big men's plates of meat up to a gargantuan size 53 (35cm), this is the shoe store for size queens, drag queens, foot fetishists and frost-bitten Big Foots alike.

The Fabulous Stringslip
Map 47, p.14
Reguliersdwarsstraat 59
+31 20 638 1143

Erotic underwear, T shirts, porn vids, dildos and other assorted party and sex gear make this a one-stop shop (pity they don't sell beer and pizza). They also sell tickets to many of the parties around town.

Trailer

Not on Map
Utrechtsestraat 139
+31 20 625 6444
www.trailer.nl

The extensive collection of sexy bedroom gear and party wear for men and women is almost an art gallery to Gothic & New Romantic fashion. Great for sitting in the back sipping coffee from their café bar & playing pirate dress-ups!

Xarina – The Latex Shop

Map 54, p.14
Singel 416 (basement)
+31 20 624 6383
Tues & Sat 11am - 5pm, Wed & Fri 11am - 6pm, Thurs 11am - 9pm
Viewing also by appointment
www.xarina.nl

Xarina has been outfitting the fabulous end of the fetish crowd here and internationally with their hand-coloured and specially made latex to produce stunning corsets, gowns and vests that shimmer like metallic reptile skins. A great selection of designs for men and women, from club wear to bridal gowns! Not just for the twisted (although taller folk will have to submit to the basement showroom's dominating low wooden beamed ceiling).

Cuts and Curls

Map 81, p.35
Korte Leidsedwarsstraat 74
Tue to Thur 10am – 8pm,
Friday till 7pm, Saturday till
4pm, Sun & Mon closed
www.cutsandcurls.com

You can find out a LOT about a town by getting your hair cut. Local gossip, what's hot, what's not. But this place in many ways also sums up Amsterdam's recent gay history. For years it was all shiny skin-heads, leather-boys and more body piercings than a St. Sebastian festival. The boys doing the best value buzzcuts in town could certainly play butch. Likewise, the salon itself tried hard to be hard-edged: a mass of rainbow and leather pride flags fluttering above a very sexy black motorcycle outside, with camouflage netting and larger-than-life-sized statues of a US Marine and LA motorcycle cop striking dramatic poses inside.

Yet lately, due to declining pink tourism and fracturing of the gay scene, the place is now half the size it once was, the pseudo-leather bar look has been stripped away and it seems more like Cuts & *Girls* since they worked out women's styling (and their perfumed products) pulls in more profit than buzzing the few old-school gay boys who aren't interested in the current just-out-of-bed look. Still the cheapest head-jobs (and best gossip) in town, it's worth waiting in line just to see some bridesmaid on a budget getting brushed down with a prickly paint brush.
NOTE: No reservations, put your name on the list at the counter and enjoy free coffee & cookies while you wait. Free WiFi & tickets to many parties available.

Fraaij

Map 63a, p.26
1st Looiersdwarsstraat 28
+31 20 427 7962
Thurs to Mon 10am till 6pm
Thurs/Fri night till 9pm
www.martijnfraaij.com

Just around the corner from über gay gym **Splash**, homos can now give their heads a good work out (no, not by actually thinking silly!) by colour specialist Martijn Fraaij. Best of all, he gives you a second washing after your cut to get rid of those annoying little hairs behind your ears!

Hotheads

Map 53a, p.14
Reguliersdwarsstraat 4
+31 20 626 8075
Tues to Sat 11am – 6pm,
Thursday till 9pm

Not gay but as it's at the top of the gay strip it gets a good amount of gay boys having bad hair days in need of a quick headjob...er, front back and sides.

Thermos Beauty Salon

Map 77, p.35
Raamdwarsstraat 5
+31 20 623 9158
Daily Noon till 8pm
www.thermos.nl

Get a haircut, beauty treatment, massage - everything from a facial to a full crack-back-and-sac-wax - in their recently renovated salon. Their expanded clothing and swimwear collection allows you to assemble a total package before taking it all off to parade the new you in their sauna around the corner.

When visiting Circuit Queens strut into **Pink Point** and ask where's good to go dancing, their faces often fall flatter than a go-go boy on GHB when they discover only the **Cockring** is open. Sadly, many gay tourists leave Amsterdam feeling our 24/7 party reputation is pretty damn pathetic. And it's true. As gay has gone global the pink tourist dollar has found cheaper and newer dance party destinations. Early in the week, and especially in winter, don't be too disappointed to discover there are more dancing queens in an ABBA musical than on the Amsterdam scene. So, as old timers grow misty-eyed reminiscing over the glory days of the **Roxy** and the **iT**, has Amsterdam's Gay Capital crown slipped so low all we're left with is a cockring?

Yet our reputation as a Gay Mecca for Muscle Marys to mechanically mince about in was never part of our deserved queer infamy. And while other, much larger and more metrosexual metropolises like Barcelona, New York or London may have surpassed Amsterdam as a party destination, how many gay dance-clubs do they have open on a Monday or Tuesday? Admittedly, the dance party scene is MUCH less dynamic and unique than it once was, but for a village of only 750,000 people the local queer folk aren't so Amster-damned after all.

However, compiling any gay dance scene list is like taking a snapshot of a cocaine bust in a cyclone. No matter where things may be now, it'll be different when the dust finally settles. Currently, there's little on offer that has any greater chance of lasting until you read this any more than other sure-fire party hits that have come and gone since the last edition. Sadder still, the women's dance events list is briefer than one of Britney's bridal parties.

So instead, before you head out futilely looking for the handful of parties we feel brave enough to list here, we recommend checking out the city-sponsored www.amsterdam4gays.com portal for all the very latest dance party and club listings, or come past Pink Point and ask us!

*NOTE: Due to recent Nazi-like crackdowns on drugs (especially GHB) expect a looooong wait in line for many clubs before getting up close and *very* personal with heavy-handed (and homophobic) security who'll feel between buttocks, cup testicles and peer down underwear (and you thought U.S. Customs was fun!).

official portal for gay Amsterdam

gay & lesbian agenda - hotels - nightlife - culture - sports

AMSTERDAM4GAYS
.com

Akhnaton

Not on Map
Nieuwezijds Kolk 25
From 9pm - early morning
ww.akhnaton.nl
Who: *Mixed Straight/Gay*
Wear: *Casual*
What ♪**:** *Varied*
When's Best: *Early*

Host to various one-off queer events including the camp **Danserette** parties, this small venue recently changed hands and had its detailed African/ethnic interior exchanged for a coat of matt black paint. At the intermittently held Danserette parties expect anything from Abba and Dutch 80s hits, to Madonna and Scissor Sisters - funny but at times painfully toe-curling.

Arabian Dance

Held irregulary. Various venues
See www.nafar.nl
Who: *Arabic, Mediterranean,*
Dutch
Wear: *From burkas to boas*
What ♪**:** *North African,*
Turkish, Middle Eastern
When's Best: *Late*

The very small Amsterdam Arabic gay community puts on these parties at various venues - check their site for the latest info. Always lots of twirling, squealing and mint tea at these events.

Asian Disco Night

@Cockring Map 12, p.24
Warmoesstraat 96
From 8pm - Midnight
www.asiandisconight.com
Every 3rd Sunday of the month
Entry €5
Who: *Asian men & friends*
Wear: *Casual*
What ♪**:** *Varied*
When's Best: *After 10*

Amsterdam's only regular party/bar for Asians and their admirers held monthly at the **Cockring**. Expect a good stirfry of Asian flavas amongst the (somewhat) older Dutch white Rice Queens as well as free snacks & 'Spectacular' surprise shows on offer. BYO chopsticks.

Club Artlaunch

Map 38b, p.15
@ Studio 80
Rembrandtplein17
Every last friday
11pm - 5 am
Entry €7
www.artlaunch.nl
Who: *Mixed gay & lesbian and some 'queer friendly' straights*
Wear: *From High Art to Camp Aesthetic*
What ♪**:** *Electro, Techno & Progressive beats*
When's Best: *Late*

In between thumping electronica sets in this unique art/music/fashion/dance party event, the first Art Launch a few years ago staged several 'art installations' by French designer & performance artist **Bondy Boy**. Dressed in a Snow White mask and black rubber catsuit, he stunned the funky queer audience (that *had* thought it'd seen it all) by having a somewhat reluctant Big Bad Wolf insert 7 red dwarf-shaped dildos up his perky butt. A fairy-story with a real twist in the end! Since then, Artlaunch have continued to shock, awe, elate and entertain Amsterdam with their innovative queer cultural swap-meets between cities like Berlin, Barcelona, Istanbul & Sao Paulo showcasing foreign funksters, performers & DJs.

Club 11

Not on Map
Oosterdokskade 3-5
www.ilove11.nl

Who: *Young groovers & late diners*

Wear: *Retro style*

What ♪**:** *Old & Nu Skool*

When's Best: *Check website for listings*

CO2

Held irregulary. Various venues
www.co2party.com

Who: *Mainly men; although apparently flicky-haired straight girls are also welcome*

Wear: *Shirtless, hairless pretty boys looking to be 'talent' scouted*

What ♪**:** *Uplifting Trance & Latin House*

When's Best: *After midnight*

Cockring

Map 12, p.24
Warmoesstraat 96
Nightly 11pm till 4am,
Friday/Saturday till 5am
Entry: €3.50, Fri/Sat €5 (sometimes MUCH higher during tourist-milking events like Pride & Queen's Day)
www.clubcockring.com

Who: *Men only; diverse, masculine mid 20s to late 30s, gym & slim*

Wear: *Jeans, tanktops or shirtless, trainers, some leather*

What ♪**:** *Hard techno downstairs. Cruisy house above*

When's Best: *After 1am Fri/Sat*

(see also: Eat - 11)

11 - the very funky restaurant/bar perched atop the soon to be demolished old Post Office building looming over Centraal Station - has an adjacent warehouse-like space that's often taken over by old skool electro-hipsters (like DJ Lupe) and their assorted queer friends. With weird and wonderful visuals on 12 huge video screens lining the walls and eclectic electro-music on the decks, it's a great place to work off the calories while hanging with Amsterdam's most metrosexual men and women.

Borrowing a concept from sun-soaked Spanish beach parties, this gig's one party trick is to blast perspiring punters with jets of cooling carbon dioxide. Yet, given that Amsterdam's venues can be plenty cold enough, only the team that (rather aptly) used an image of a lemon to advertise a recent **Orange Ball** could consider air-conditioning much of a 'sensation.' Luckily, decent music keeps the punters happily working up a sweat. After a few lacklustre gay events (ie: a most vanilla Black Party), promoter Robert Riedijk has lost considerable ground to parties such as **Rapido**, so he craftily avoids marketing this gig as his own. Finally he's hit upon a simple but successful formula: danceable DJs, performers and fashion shows that *don't* interrupt the music, reasonable entry prices and dropping the ego-trip that once splashed his name across every one of his colour-themed parties.

(see also: Drink - Leather)

They used to sell nitrous oxide balloons here, giving gay boys even lighter heads and making the place look like Chuckles the Clown stopped in after a kiddies party. The balloons are gone but the party mood remains, largely due to the 'Ring's late closing hours, good hard music and late-night punters wanting to keep on dancing with few other choices. Formerly an infamous leather bar, now all types invariably end up in this compact 3 level club, rubbing against each other in on the tiny dance floor or bumping and grinding to a different tune in the darkroom & cubicles upstairs.

Beware of pickpockets in the darker corners, the dreaded stairs if you've had one too many drinks and the *"live sex shows"* (every Thursday, Friday & Sunday) are live only in the sense that you can actually see the so-called "*international porn stars*" breathing. Often jam-packed on the weekends (adding to the cruisy feeling), it's the perfect place for those into frottage - but not for claustrophobiacs or those with a fire-trap phobia. Early in the week however, it's more tourists than locals making even the postage-stamp sized dancefloor disappointingly quiet.

Epicentre

@ Studio 80 Map 38b, p.15
Held irregularly
Entry: €7.50
www.epicentre-amsterdam.nl
Who: *Mixed; Men & Women all scarily young (16+)*
Wear: *Gothic, Fetish, Cyber, Alt (anything really, so long as it's black!)*
What ♪: *Gothic, Darkwave, Electro, EBM & Industrial*
When's Best: *Midnight (duh!)*

If your taste in bars and clubs lean less to the light and fluffy and more to the dark and *'Buffy'* then those with blackened souls (and even blacker eyeliner) can sink their pointy teeth into like-minded goth boys and goul girls at this harder-edged club for those with heaving hormones. With an age limit of 16 years & up some of the raven-haired ravers here seem less undead than new born, but they do go about partying like baby bats out of hell with virginal eardrums to sacrifice at the booming Industrial/Darkwave altar. And since moving from the now defunct COC building to a more grown-up venue this party is no longer just for gay goths and willowy wiccas but is still very queer friendly.

Exit

Map 48, p.14
Reguliersdwarsstraat 42
Wed, Thurs, Sun: 11pm – 4am
Friday/Saturday 11pm – 5am
Entry €5 - €7
www.clubexit.eu
Who: *Mainly men; diverse, mid 20s to 30s, women welcome*
Wear: *Stylish & trendy*
What ♪: *Varied (R&B, Pop, House, Techno & Trance)*
When's Best: *After Midnight*

Exit's like that old fuck buddy you call in on every now and again when there's nothing better available. For 17 years this cramped wooden-beamed place (looking more like it should be a leather bar) has been pumping out the same tried and true formula and, being the only gay club on the pink strip, it has a certain monopoly on drinkers who want to dance off a few too many dacquiris. A good place to go if you're with a bunch of mates whose CDs you'd never borrow even if there were no drink coasters in the house. When in full swing this venue has different musical styles across 4 levels, so there should be something for almost everyone. The dance floor gernally pumps commercial techno tracks, while the adjacent bars (the balcony & 1st floor) play 'happy house', R&B and commercial 'urban vibes'. Accordingly, the crowd (mostly toursists) can be interestingly diverse and there's even a darkroom in the attic for dancing of the... er, dirtier kind.
Also hosts monthly lesbian dance party **Garbo**.

Fresh

(see: Dance - Generic Circuit party)

Furball

Every 6 weeks
@ Club Exit, Map 48, p.14
Reguliersdwarsstraat 42
11pm - 4am
Entry: €6
Online reservations for visitors outside Holland
www.furball.nl
Who: *Men only*
Wear: *Shoulder, back, chest hair*
What ♪: *Teddy-Bear's Picnic?*
When's Best: *After 12*

Since Amsterdam hacked up it's first Furball in 2005 this party for the heavier and hirsute homo has become one of the hottest and (thankfully!) attitude-free parties in town (with nary a pumped-up disco twink high on GHB and self-importance in sight). Not just for cuddly Gentle Bens who get off watching shaving fetish videos in rewind, the High-School-Ball-meets-Care-Bear-convention feel of the now defunct COC building has grown up into a seriously sexy gig for cubs, otters, wolves, pandas, musclebears, chasers, admirers and more assorted woolly woodland creatures than an Ewok family reunion.

(Cont.)

Furball
(cont.)

But like all cubs, the day arrived for it to go hunting for a new home when the COC's closure sent it out into the wilderness, with it yet to find a regular home of its own. The always warm, fuzzy attitude of the crowd and the energy of its hard-working volunteers however, seems to be able to transform even the most cold and claustrophobic venues into a cosy cave, but after the ill-considered crush of the Supperclub's basement its reputation bearly survived. Recently relocated to the disjointed disco Exit (with its furry fan base grizzling about the hairless twink porn vids on display) many worried that this party would soon be yet another head on the trophy wall of extinct Amsterdam clubs. But with Mr Furball competitions planned for the infinitely improved Melkweg, perhaps we won't have to grin and bear it for too much longer.

(Generic Circuit Party)

Could be anywhere on Map
Who: *Mainly men; shirtless, hairless gym queens with perfect teeth, razor-sharp tanlines & pupils like railway tunnels. Women welcome (although totally ignored!)*
Wear: *Bare chests & jeans barely above the pubic bone, some glam*
What ♪: *Happy handbag to heavier house & techno*
When's Best: *Check flyers & gay mags*

Amsterdam's dance party promoters have a great insight into the human condition; particularly the Gay Goldfish memory syndrome. Despite bitching about having the same thing dished out month after month, Amsterdam's Attention Deficit Disorder boys seem happy to swim around the same buffed body of water so long as the gig changes its name as regularly as they do their boyfriends. No matter if it's the same promotor pumping out the same party so long as the disco tits stay perky.

Rapido (named after the speed tickets sell out) is currently so hot that desperately late punters have been known to bid hundreds of Euros on Ebay to muscle up with the other Marys inside Paradiso's hallowed halls. Run by Spain's spectacularly successful Matinee Group this party manages to mix the best of Ibiza-style music in a former church along the Singel canal. An old revival-hall with old-worlde charm, Paradiso has a big wooden floored dance area (believe me, this is a HUGE plus!), a great variety of smaller spaces up and down stairs (great for when that E hits and you start doing a "Just keep swimming" Dory impersonation) and plenty of good vantage points to check out the always sexy crowd from the balustraded balcony. Look out for their occasional Beach editions in Summer.

While **Reflexxx** (in collaboration with Matinee) with its vocal, happy power house seems to be just another name for the same old circuit party that's always been held in Escape - the biggest club venue on Rembrandtplein - it's probably already changed names by the time you read this.

(Cont.)

(Generic Circuit Party)
(cont.)

Finally, **Fresh** (the kid brother of Rapido organised by - you guessed it! - the Matinee monopoly) - is a monthly (every 1st Fri) gig for those who prefer their parties up close and personal. The glassed in area at the back of the upstairs bar in Escape only holds a few hundred at best and can be kinda weird with the straight regular joes at Escape peering in for a perve but it's funky and progressive house always gives it a good vibe. Entrance through the Escape's delightful fire escape at Amstel 80.

*NOTE: Due to the **Escape** being nailed shut some years back after a police drug bust (that left the floor looking whiter than Michael Jackson's complexion), they now have an (at times) quite aggressive, heavy-handed and rather homophobic frisking and body cavity search policy. Normally I prefer being bought a drink *before* my first grope!

Grey Pink
Map 21a, p.24
@ Paleis van de Weemoed
Oudezijds Voorburgwal 15
+31 20 625 6964
Every first Wednesday
Entry: €7.50 **(Cont.)**

The new hang-out for the older, balding & blue-rinse set, this monthly party organised in cooperation with **Artlaunch** for greying gays (and lesbians) has DJs playing nostalgic hits and shows appropriate for a more than mature audience. Friendly and fun, people from all ages are welcome.

FURBALL
THE AMSTERDAM
HAIRY MEN
DANCE PARTY

Muscle Bears
Hairy Men
Bears
Otters
Cubs
Smooth
Admirers

WWW.FURBALL.NL

Grey Pink (cont.)

Who: *40+ mostly male, women welcome*

Wear: *Finally, a place where you can dress your age!*

What ♪**:** *Nostalgia & 70s Disco hits*

When's Best: *After that midlife crisis*

Joystick

Not on Map
Vak Zuid, Olympisch Stadion 35
Entry: €20 presale - €25 door
Held irregularly
www.joystick-amsterdam.com

Who: *Mostly men, women welcome*

Wear: *Tanktops at most, jeans & army pants*

What ♪**:** *Happy handbag & vocal tunes to heavier house & techno*

When's Best: *Get there early to avoid the security line up*

Melkweg

Not on Map
Lijnbaansgracht 234a
+31 20 531 8181
www.melkweg.nl

Who: *Mainly straight, but queer friendly crowd*

Wear: *Varied*

What ♪**:** *Check web site*

When's Best: *Check web site*

Paradiso

Not on Map
Weteringschans 6-8
+31 20 626 45 21
www.paradiso.nl

Who: *Mainly straight, but queer friendly crowd*

Wear: *Varied*

What ♪**:** *Check web site*

When's Best: *Check web site*

Rapido

For more info check out:
www.artlaunch.nl/paleis/pvdwinfo.html

When Amsterdam's rather constipated gay dance scene looked in dire need of a high-powered colonic a few years back, along came the invading Germans with their wonderful Joystick to get everything moving again. Since 2004 this mega party added much needed roughage to Amsterdam's formerly meagre dance diet. Sadly, like so many other clubs it began to falter, losing favour to newer parties like Rapido and disappeared in 2006. Recently revived by new management R&D Productions and relocated to Amsterdam's great old Olympic Stadium, only time will tell if this stick still holds any lasting joy (and if punters are willing to be bussed out to the 'burbs).

A real Amsterdam institution, this former milk factory next to the Leidseplein houses concerts, exhibitions, a coffeeshop and parties. Not a gay venue as such, they do however, host occasional one-off gay parties (like **White Party** and **Furball**) as well as many other gay-friendly events during the year.

An old revival hall style church converted in 1968 into a publicly-subsidised youth entertainment centre, Paradiso has become one of Amsterdam's best and most versatile venues. Staging intimate rock gigs, theatre, classical performances, lectures, benefits and the occassional gay dance party (**Rapido** and **Lovedance**) this place is a must for anyone who likes to see a show up close in olde-worlde charm. Keith Richards from the Rolling Stones reckons their concerts (recorded for their *Stripped* album) were their best live shows ever (although Richards remembering anything he did in Amsterdam of all places is a bit of a reach!).

(see: Generic Circuit party)

Spellbound

@ OCCII
Not on Map
Amstelveenseweg 134
Saturday every 2 months
11pm till 4am
€7 entry
www.spellbound-amsterdam.nl

Who: *Mixed; Alternative queer men & women*

Wear: *Retro, skins, goths, punks. some leather*

What ♪ **:** *Hard Techno/Electro Grunge*

When's Best: *Midnight*

Once every two months this former squat on the other side of **Vondel Park** is assimilated by the **Spellbound** Queer collective. Their alternative parties are like those artsy student things you used to go to while ignoring University classes. Enjoyable coz they're not like anything else you'd been to, while at the same time you'd nervously wonder, *"who are all these weird fucks, what the fuck is this music, and when are the police going to shut it down and take us all in for questioning?"* Sure the music can be (at times) atrocious and ear-bleedingly deafening and the décor straight out of post war Berlin, but this party is hugely popular amongst those funky Amsterdam queers that break out in a rash just looking at an Abercrombie & Fitch catalogue. From androgynous boys in their grandma's Sunday best, to bulldykes performing drag-king versions of Christ's Crucifixion on stage (and LOTS of funky good looking guys and grrrls who don't think 'gay' means having to be 'straight-acting', or go to a gym every day, shave their body hair or use a solarium). Expect every variant of queer expression, one of the cheapest places for beer and the chilled upstairs vodka bar plays some seriously funky retro and electro-clash tracks.

SPECIAL EVENTS:
Spellbound organises various underground parties in other locations like **Flush It** (motto "The best parties always happen in the toilets!") and **Disco Hospital**. Check website for venues and dates.

Stetsons

Not on Map
Zuiderzeeweg
Zeeburgereiland
www.stetsons.nl
Mon: 7:30 - 10:30pm
Tue: 8 - 10:30pm
Membership €6/month

Who: *Mixed; men & women*

Wear: *Cowboy style*

What ♪ **:** *Country & Western*

When's Best: *Cockroach season*

(see also: Gay Western Saloon - Special Events)
Ok, most gay boy's only admiration for line dancing stops at those cute cowboys back of Madonna in her *'Don't Tell Me'* clip. But since 1993, there's been a sizable group of locals skooting their boots every Monday (advanced) & Tuesday (Jedi master) at Amsterdam's first (and only) Country & Western dance club for gays & lesbians. Mostly line dancing, with some circle & partner dances, they also hold occassional beginner's classes when there's enough numbers - all are made welcome. Look out for occasional **Gay Western Saloon** parties.

Studio 80

Map 38b, p.15
Rembrandtplein 17
Nightly
www.studio-80.nl
Who: *Mixed; men & women, often gay and or queer friendly*
Wear: *Casual (but basic black never fails!)*
What ♪: *Varied*
When's Best: *Check web site*

Great new-ish venue on Rembrandtplein that immediately became hot when it opened its doors a few years back. Lots of gay mixed, gay friendly or just gay gay events here.

SPECIAL EVENTS:
F*cking Pop Queers - Wednesdays from 11 myspace.com/popqueers - Pop night from Madonna to indie, electro and urban
Club Artlaunch - Every fourth Friday (see separate listing)
Epicentre - see separate listing

Sugar Factory

Map 77a, p.35
Lijnbaansgracht 238
Thursday to Sunday
Entry price varies
11pm - 5am
www.sugarfactory.nl
Who: *Mixed; Straight/Gay*
Wear: *Funky*
What ♪: *Anything!*
When's Best: *Take your pick*

Sporting more personalities than a *Dancing With The Stars* Christmas special, this 'night theatre' is a cross between a dance club, cabaret, art gallery, music hall, performance space and metrosexual museum. Established by members of the Winston Hotel (DJ Polack & partner Mzzz Erin Tasmania - surely a Drag Queen trapped in an Aussie chick's body!), the always entertaining and inventive line-up aims to take art out of the museums to highlight bands, DJs, fashion, poetry and other funky performances as supreme human expression.

SPECIAL EVENTS:
Club Cut: Bi-monthly queer friendly dance party with latin house, vocals & feel good house beats.
Vreemd: Meaning 'strange' in Dutch, this weekly mixed gay/straight club night features somewhat strange DJs, VJs art & performances (and its once a month party **Wildvreemd** can get really strange).
Girlesque: Occasional women's party organised by the old **Venus Freaks** collective.

Supperclub

Map 56b, p.14
Jonge Roelensteeg 21
+31 20 344 6400
www.supperclub.nl
Who: *Mixed; but always queer friendly*
Wear: *Casual-chic to stylish sleaze*
What ♪: *Varied*
When's Best: *Check web site*

(see also: Eat - Restaurants)
Super cool dining experience Supperclub has always prided itself on its musical credentials having released over 10 CDs of suitably chilled tracks and having many a DJ spin their platters after the plates have been wiped clean. But now they seem keen to further their Queer credentials by sometimes tinting their big white space pink.

SPECIAL EVENTS:
Dirty Dancing: Free party every last Friday of the month.
Sphincter: The delightfully named monthly Tea Dance every 1st Sunday (for those old enough to have worn out their own!)
Supperclub Cruise: A fabulous floating fun palace operating in Summer months only.

Trut

(see: Drink - Funky & Alternative)

Unk

@ Club 8 (Not on Map)
Admiral de Ruyterweg 56
Every 4th Sat night
Entry €8
11pm - 4am
www.djlupe.com
Who: *Mixed; queer friendly*
Wear: *Funky*
What ♪: *Electro stuff*
When's Best: *After 12*

You II

Map 34, p.15
Amstel 178
Thurs 10pm till 4am
Fri/Sat till 5am
www.youii.nl
Who: *Mainly women early,*
gay men after 1am
Wear: *Casual*
What ♪: *Top 40*
When's Best: *Friday &*
Saturday after 1am

Somewhat removed from the inner-city gay ghettos, next to a discount supermarket & above a somewhat seedy pool hall the utterly unpretentious Unk is not what you'd ever call glam. Neither would its alternative queer organisers care for the title - they'd rather just add the letters 'F', 'P' (or even 'J' & 'Dr') to their name for more apt descriptions. Always eclectic but entertaining music from DJs Lupe & LAVA, a broad cross section of Amsterdam's non-Guppie men & women and a good-natured feel make this place a worthwhile tram ride.

The increasingly aptly-named You II has been displaying distinct dual personalities of late. During the week and early evenings weekends this intimate, olde-world nightclub with its fab, faux Art Nouveau stained glass lighting boasts more pussy fanciers than a cat groomers convention. But on weekends after midnight it's more and more of a chicken farm as the baby gays bar-crawling along the **Amstel** finally make it up river (with the odd late-night rent boy all dressed up with no one to blow). Ironically, the more it bulges with boys the less butch it becomes as the Diesel Dykes take their brawling home. Recently taken over by the owner of **Arc**, this seems to be one Sybil that may soon (sadly) sever its sisterhood personalities forever.

Flirtation

@ Panama (Not on Map)
Oostelijke Handelskade 4
11pm till 4am
Entry: €15 (online only)
www.letsbeopen.nl

Who: Women only; younger lipstick types

Wear: Themed dresscode

What ♪ **:** Dance in main hall, R&B in studio.

Celebrating its 4th year in 2007 these mega 'girls night out' parties held 5 times a year (by former Big Brother winner Bianca) have been hugely successful and show the gay boys a thing or two about staging a fab, friendly and fun event with great female DJs, live acts and always impressively-themed decorations. Tickets always sell out fast so order yours online fast.

Garbo

@ Strand West (Not on Map)
Stavangerweg 900
Every 1st Saturday
Entry €5
www.garboforwomen.nl
@ Exit
Map 48, p.14
Reguliersdwarsstraat 42
Every 4th Sunday
Entry €4.50
www.garboinexit.nl

Who: Women only

Wear: Casual

What ♪ **:** 70s & 80s

When's Best: Late

Depending on your proclivities, celebrating your 1 year anniversary may not be much to write about but in the fragile and fickle Amsterdam women's dance scene 12 months is an impressive milestone. Organised by volunteers this friendly Women-only dance event is held every 1st Saturday of the month at the rather classy (but somewhat distant docklands lounge venue) **Strand West** and every 4th Sunday of every month at the rather non-classy (but centre of boystown) **Exit** disco. This is one Garbo that isn't going to be left alone.

Girlesque

@ Sugar Factory
Map 77a, p.35
www.venusfreaks.nl

Who: Mostly women, men welcome with female friend

Wear: Bawdy & Burlesque

What ♪ **:** Diverse

When's Best: Check web site

Girlesque is an occasional women's party held in the **Sugar Factory** and organised by the infamous party grrls behind the now legendary (and sadly missed) **Venus Freaks**. Celebrating shameless, yet still stylish burlesque, it's a sweaty, swinging club for good girls bent bad (and gay boys who want to borrow the fish nets & feather boas). Men welcome in the company of a female friend (or two). Also check **www.sugarfactory.nl** for agenda.

Sappho	(see: Drink – Lesbian Bars)
Spellbound	(see: Dance)
De Trut	(see: Drink - Funky & Alternative)
Unk	(see: Dance)
You II	(see: Previous page)

Gay Western Saloon

@ Crea Café Map 30b, p.14
Grimburgwal
www.stetsons.nl
Entry €5

Who: *Cowboys & Cowgrrrls*
Wear: *44 gallon hats, jeans*
& boots
What ♪**:** *Both kinds of music:*
country & western

Tired of dull, souless dance music? Since '98 Amsterdam's first (and to our knowledge *only*) dance club for gays and lesbians who'd rather stamp their feet to Tammy, Dolly & Shania than Kylie or Madge. Novice and experienced line dancers (mostly from **Stetsons**) are welcome. But if you let your partner lead, does that make you a bottom?

Various events held throughout the year including Valentine's Day, Gay Pride, Halloween & Christmas.

Black Party

Not on map
www.riedijkproductions.com
Entry €25 (approx.)

Who: *Walk-on-the-wild-side wannabes*
Wear: *Apparently blue jeans are considered black enough*
What ♪**:** *Half-way decent hard house (finally!)*
When's best: *Maybe next time?*

The sexy African-American sporting a white stripe down his skin tight leather pants most summed up Robert Riedijk's Black Party. When asked what fetish the stripe indicated he responded: "Nothing. I'm not into anything in particular". Likewise, this party also has the same Oreo Cookie quality: black on the outside but pure vanilla within. SM here simply means Stand & Model. Not surprisingly, the few hardcore fetish folk that attended peered down their pierced noses bitching it was about as black as Michael Jackson's butt cheeks. Yet, for the softer core - attracted by the success of Riedijk's White Parties & inventively dresssed in black T shirts & jeans - the sight of the few hairy men in chaps & harnesses soon had these disco Dairy Queens nervously dripping under their thin chocolate coatings. Not the best pairing for a good night out.

For Riedijk to resurrect his Black Party after a well-deserved absence (cue scary flashback of Lamahl's *Never Ending Story* at the disasturous 2003 edition), you'd think he'd have learned from past mistakes. But sparing all expense and originality by simply putting together a poor facsimile of the XXXL party formula, the poor attendance (including a laughably empty and *white* leatherette VIP area) and pitifully small play areas proved he'll have few fetish fans - black or white - next time. At least he scores points for more than decent music & emblazoning his name across the DJ booth to help those who did bother to turn up not make the same mistake twice.

Lovedance

@ Paradiso
Not on Map
December 1
Who: *Amsterdam's finest*
"stars & freaks"
Wear: *Red Ribbons*
What ♪**:** *Funky & very varied*

Combining the talents and energy of virtually every gay organisation in town, this is a hugely popular and immensely worthy **AIDS Fonds** benefit party that always sells out weeks before (so get your tickets early). Bringing out a great cross-section of Amsterdam's "stars & freaks" and every other type of queer this "full night extravaganza" is as much a celebration of survival as a commemoration of those we've all lost. An almost disturbingly diverse list of acts and performances makes staying in one spot almost impossible, but as it's the place to be seen, it makes the metrosexual mingling amidst the various rooms filled with fashion, art, speeches and good amounts of dancing a must.

A special mention must be given to one-time Disco Diva CC Peniston's utmost professionalism while belting out her hit *Finally* a few years back. Almost choking on a bit of bracelet that flew into her mouth she stopped mid-tune, tossed aside the gagging glitter and (finally!) gave her finale while two drag queens in front of the stage wrestled for the offending bling. Now that's class!

Orange Ball

Various Venues
Night before Queen's Day
9pm – till 4:30am
Entry €25 (approx)
www.riedijkproductions.com
Who: *Mainly men; women welcome*
Wear: *Anything orange*
What ♪**:** *Happy Techno*

Think **White Party** after you've spilled a large bottle of Fanta. With everyone sporting the Dutch Royal house colour this is a friendly, boppy 'circuit party' style event, held in a different venue every year (to varying success). Still, going into its 8th year, and as one of *the* annual parties on the Amsterdam queer social calendar, it's a chance to catch up with virtually everyone in town, no matter what true colours they normally fly.

White Party

Various venues
First Saturday in August (after Canal Parade)
11pm – till late
Entry €22 presale, €29 at door
www.whiteparty.nl
Who: *Mainly men; women welcome*
Wear: *Like a toothpaste commercial*
What ♪**:** *Happy House & Techno*

These parties not only look like soap powder commercials but everyone also (mostly) behaves as squeaky clean as Bree Van De Kamp on a bad hair day. Why is it when everyone wears white they're too afraid to get down and dirty? Difficult to budge knee stains? Still, the lack of any real sexual energy is offset by the general happy mood everyone's in, the boppy music and the fact everyone's summer tans look fabulous in contrast to all the sparkling white outfits. But like all whites with a few too many spins in the wash (since debuting in '96), this is yet another Riedijk outfit showing disturbing signs of going grey. Still, you have to hand it to Riedijk for persevering when many other promoters have simply faded away. Staging his 10th Anniversary White Party in 2007 he must be doing something white…er, right.

FUCK

While it's true there's no 'pay-per-view' gay sex shows in town, it's because there's so much on offer for free! So, if you're after a perverted performance (and like living dangerously), simply take a torch into one of the many darkrooms and play spaces of Amsterdam's fantastic fetish scene (then prepare to run like all fuck!).

Those who prefer to take their clothes off *before* they meet a tall, dark stranger are well catered for with a busy steam room, spa bath or gym change room virtually in every corner of the city (special mention going to the infamous shower and sauna scenes at the **Splash** fitness clubs).

For any Grrrl-on-Grrrl action it's pretty slim pickings (if you discount the straight fantasy lesbo-scenes often displayed amidst the mixed fetish parties and Red-Light District shows where 2 bored bimbos twist each other's nipples like they're trying to tune into Radio Free Europe). However, look out for occasional SM workshops by lesbian group **WildSide**.

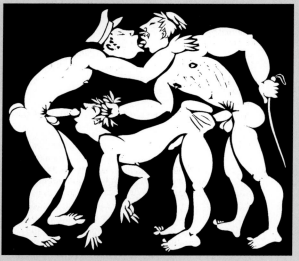

Lastly, while Safe Sex is still being officially promoted (although mostly only in the **Take Care - Living PositHIV** awareness week leading up to **World AIDS Day**), finding condoms and lube (as well as even hygiene basics like soap and paper towels) is, in many sex-on-premises venues, often harder than the member you'll be using them on. So make sure you stock up before you head out. STD's are *not* souvenirs you'll want to take home to show your Mother!

Men Only Parties (Safe Sex only)

NIGHTLY

Jack Off Parties

@ Stablemaster
Map 21, p.24
Warmoesstraat 23
+31 20 625 0148
Thurs-Monday open from 9pm
Tuesday/Wednesday closed
www.stablemaster.nl

Who: *Men only; mixed ages to slighty older crowd*

Wear: *Naked*

What ♪: *Happy slapping noises (just like boarding school nights)*

These small parties (maximum capacity is about 40) can nevertheless be sexy and a lot of fun. The bar is decked out in a country-and-western style but luckily, with none of those itchy hay bales lying about! Although officially a JO party, punters have been known to take on more than just (ahem) the matter at hand. Only problem is how to hold a beer glass with greasy hands. Dress code is naked.

WEEKLY

Sameplace

Nassaukade 120 (Not on Map)
Monday 8pm till 1am
Entry: €5 - Free before 10pm
www.sameplace.nl

Who: *Men only*

Wear: *One piece of clothing (you choose)*

What ♪: *Diverse*

If Sunday has come and gone but *you've* yet to cum, this "after weekend sex party" may be just the thing to clear the pipes. Being just outside the city centre, and officially a *Men Only* function (not a Gay night - if you get the subtle distinction) this weekly 'Boner Night' draws an altogether different crowd, including the odd tranny (which is a very hard act as guests are only allowed to wear one piece of clothing!).

SPECIAL EVENTS:
Sunny Gay Day every 4th Sunday 3-7pm
Transgender & Transexual Night every 3rd Wed 8pm

EVERY 2 WEEKS

S.O.S. – Sex on Sunday

@ Eagle
Map 14, p.24
Warmoesstraat 90
Second and last Sunday of the month, 4pm – 8pm
Entry: €7

Who: *Men only*

Wear: *Shirtless or nude*

What ♪: *Diverse & perverse*

It's a weird feeling walking into a bar all rugged up against the chilly Amsterdam winds, only to find yourself amidst a room full of naked guys sitting chatting with mates as if the Emperor's new tailor is the only place to shop. These hot and horny afternoon parties are always pretty busy with plenty of action going on (and not just in the downstairs darkroom!) but they're also friendly and relaxed. Those not wanting to let it all hang out can go topless and keep their modesty intact (and other shortcomings unrevealed). Organised by non-profit group **GALA**, Safe Sex activities are promoted and guests are welcome to help themselves to plentiful condoms and lube.

FF Party

@ Eagle
Map 14, p.24
Warmoesstraat 90
First Sunday of the month
3pm – 9pm
€11 entry, members €10
www.xs4all.nl/~theeagle/
Who: *Men only*
Wear: *Greasy chaps and gloves*
What ♫: *Oink Oink*

If you don't know what FF stands for, you probably shouldn't be attending this one. Go home and read *'Farewell to Arms'* instead. The slew of slings downstairs see more handball action than an Olympic Games demonstration sport and the sling above the pool table upstairs is for those that don't just want to make eyeballs pop.

*NOTE: Bring your own Crisco (but this ain't no cherry-pie bake-off kids!), and, as a small word of warning, the free popcorn on the bar has probably had more fingers in it than you'll *ever* have. Lastly, shamefully, you'll also need to arm yourself with a bar of soap and paper towels as the Eagle doesn't even think providing warm water to wash up with necessary at such an event. But why does acting piggy mean you have to put up with this shit? You'd be better off making the trek to Eindhoven and checking out the inffinitely better run Vagevuur (www.vagevuur.com).

Golden Shower Parties

@ Dirty Dicks
Map 15, p.24
Warmoesstraat 86
Last Thurs of the month
Who: *Men only*
Wear: *Drip dry fabrics*
What ♫: *Singing in the Rain*

Amsterdam's weather virtually necessitates wet-weather gear to be close at hand all year round, but Gene Kelly may well turn over in his grave if he knew what gay antics were happening under these downpours. No brolly necessary!

Horsemen and Knights

@ Cockring
Map 12, p.24
Warmoesstraat 96
Third Sunday of the month
Enter between 3pm – 4pm.
Open until 7pm
Entry: €8 Horsemen free
www.ncadam.com
Who: *Men only*
Wear: *Naked or underwear*
What ♫: *Sadly, rarely the sound of jaws hitting the floor*

What's that joke about Prince Charles wanting a 12 inch dick just so everyone would call him a ruler? No, we're not talking jodhpurs and riding crops fellas. Those endowed with members 18cm (that's 7 inches to you old imperialists) and above get to register their private members as permanent members - for free. If you think you might qualify as a 'horseman' get yourself measured with the 'peter-meter' (oh, to have that kind of repetitive work injury!). The rest of us non-horsemen (would that be Shetland Pony men?) are also graciously welcomed. Where else but a gay party would you still be considered overdressed wearing only your underwear?

photo www.manopoly.com

Nude Club Adam

@ Cockring
Map 12, p.24
Warmoesstraat 96
First Sunday of the month
Enter between 3-4 pm, open
until 7 pm
€8 entry
www.ncadam.com
Who: *Men only*
Wear: *Footwear only*
What ♪**:** *Cruisy techno*

Another of the testosterone parties, which always draw pretty much a full house. Action on all three levels, the dance floor, bar and darkroom. *"Kissing, sucking and fucking are the order of the day. But do it safely or you will be asked to leave and never be allowed in again"* from the NCA website, pretty much says it all.

SPECIAL EVENTS:
NC Adam also hosts **Sportswear** theme parties throughout the year - check flyers, www.amsterdam4gays.com, or ask at **Pink Point** for more details.

SEMI REGULAR

Empire

@ The Vault
Not on Map
Prins Hendrikkade 194
7pm – Midnight
Presale tix €15 – Door €20
www.empireparty.punt.nl
Who: *Men only*
Wear: *Leather, latex and uniform only. No jeans, camouflage or sportswear.*
What ♪**:** *Hard n Horny Techno*
When's Best: *After 12*

Why are so many sex events held in out-of-hours laser gun venues? I mean, who finds these places? Some perverted parent takes their kids out for the day, finds themselves with something looking like a gun in their pocket in a darkened room and suddenly the lightbulb goes off over their heads: Hey I could have some real fun in here if the age limit was raised a little!

Held in a basement laser game zone just down from Centraal Station this low key sex party took everyone who attended it pleasantly by surprise. Nobody had heard of it or the venue before, few knew anything about the organisers, and from the look of both the flyers and the hastily put together website, the expected amateurism was in fact run very professionally. (Note to other party promoters: sometimes it pays to not give punters too high an expectation).

A roomy 400 square metres of dungeons, darkrooms, glory holes, slings, crosses, cages and more bondage gear than a cross Atlantic cruise by the Dutch East India Company was soon filled by a good amount of horny and hunky men who all would've preferred the half-way decent music from DJ Jarb to be playing where the horizontal dancing was taking place rather than the postage-sized (yet still deserted) dancefloor above.

Trash

Various venues
www.clubtrash.com

Who: *Men only*

Wear: *Strict dress code: leather, rubber, uniform, fetish, skinhead, naked. No sports-wear!*

What ♪**:** *Hard n Horny Techno*

When's Best: *Maybe next time?*

Ever heard of the 'Three strikes and you're out' policy? We need it introduced to the sex-party scene with Club Trash top of the warnings list. While years ago the ever-popular **MegaTrash** parties fanned Amsterdam's infamy as a fetish fantasy city (where else could you see a **Mr Leather Europe** finalist being punch-fisted while singing Pavarotti!), it seemed the promoter could do no wrong.

That is, until MegaTrash III, when 1,500 leather boys - all peaking as one - discovered the venue's unpublicised early 3am licence meant lights glaring and orders blaring to bus it across town to another venue. Turning uglier than a Republican party convention, the mob left the cloakroom looking like a Macy's Sale after too much Crystal Meth. STRIKE ONE! Then in 2005, their much hyped Perverts party dumped punters in a western suburbs reception centre that felt about as horny as humping in your Grandma's retirement home. STRIKE TWO!

Returning a year later to a relatively inner-city (but no less dreary) party centre, Club Trash seemed to be slowly resurrecting it's reputation with small-scale, semi-regular sex parties that neither offended nor went off (although the musty army nets hanging in the darkroom next to candles artfully decorating a floor primed with spilt poppers could've made things MUCH hotter!). But with recent last-minute cancellations, critical comments about pricing and a one condom per customer policy the parties seemed even more amateurish than the artwork on their flyers. Now promising new management and staff for (yet another!) relaunch, is the gay gavel poised to finally take out this trash?

XXXLeather

Various venues
Entry €20 - €25 at door
www.xxxleather.eu

Who: *Men only*

Wear: *Strict dress code - Leather, Uniform, Rubber & Skin only (no jeans, total nudity or only jockstraps)*

What ♪**:** *Hard n Horny Techno*

When's Best: *After Midnight*

Late 2004 the **COC** (Amsterdam's outdated gay rights organistation displaying the kind of wisdom that would eventually see it close altogether) decided to fuck up its hugely popular **Leather/Rubber/SM** parties by fucking over their hard-working volunteers. Instead of taking it up the arse the volunteers formed the **Gents Foundation** and put together their own fetish party XXXLeather (triple X's neatly standing for X-rated, Xtra Large and Amsterdam's Coat of Arms).
Proving a well-run and well-thought out leather party and play space could attract a horny crowd (that normally get nose bleeds when venturing outside the Ring Road) to a venue 30 minutes drive outside of Amsterdam, the XXXL parties were so incredibly popular even long-standing fetish giant **Playgrounds** decided to simply copy the winning formula with its 2005 party at the same venue.

(Cont.)

XXXLeather
(cont.)

They even upstaged Leather Pride's Playgrounds party (and somewhat revived Amsterdam's lagging leather reputation) by staging the **Mr Leather Europe** competition to a packed crowd whipped into a frenzy by the Danish entrant who finished his fantasy element by unfurling the flags of all nations from within his perky (but apparently UN Assembly hall-sized) arse (only to lose the Top prize sash for being too blatant a bottom!).

But the long bus trips home finally took their toll, and XXXL moved briefly back into town to the aptly named Club More, only to have it change owners and go anti-gay a few months later. At the time of writing this party is still to find a permanent home but the hard-working volunteers ensure us they'll be back with an even bigger and badder version at a new venue soon.

ANNUAL

Playgrounds
*Secret location
(shuttlebuses to venue)
Late Oct/Early Nov
www.leatherpride.nl*
Who: *Men only*
Wear: *Friday: Fetish Lite
(check website for details)
Saturday: Leather/Heavy Fetish*
What ♫**:** *Heavy trance/house*
When's Best: *Saturday*

Ever get one of those report cards saying you *"played well with others"*? Well, if you're into the smell of leather and the whiff of semi-public perversions, early winter in Amsterdam is *the* place for your next outing. The short school bus-like journey to a secret location may make the youngsters aboard feel like entering holding hands two-by-two. But on arrival, leave your coat and innocence at the door. Inside, cross a dance party with an all-ages orgy, deck everyone out in remnants from the '*Matrix*' trilogy and let them run amok in a warehouse filled with twisted play equipment (as if designed by *Bob the Builder* with erections of an entirely different kind in mind) for horned-up kids on way too much jungle juice to scramble over.

Yet this long-standing highlight on a leather lowlife's calendar has struggled to meet its own well-deserved reputation recently. Unable to find the industrial locations of past years in 2006 they had to settle for a less than satisfactory family fun centre that had a bar decked out in what looked like a Bavarian ski lodge and a play area in a confusing laser gun maze (where distressed kiddies are no doubt still stumbling across bound and gagged gimps forgotten by their masters in the darker nooks and crannies).

However, these parties still draw in a good, sexy crowd out to behave badly with their new-found friends. If you told your folks you were visiting Amsterdam this is the sort of thing your Mother's been having nightmares about ever since.

Darkrooms

Adonis (Sex shop & Porn Cinema)
Action behind the screen.

Argos (Bar)
Downstairs, past toilets on the mezzanine level.

B1 (Sex shop & Porn Cinema)
Extensive dark room and glory hole areas on 2nd & 3rd floor (1st floor straight porn).

Cockring (Bar & Dance club)
On 3rd floor up the stairs at the back of bar - now with private cabins & 'body button' system.

Cuckoo's Nest (Bar)
Downstairs, past the bar.

Dirty Dick's (Bar)
Backroom, past the bar and toilets.

Drakes (Sex shop)
Upstairs video cabins all have ample ventilation holes!

Eagle (Bar)
Downstairs, past the bar. Sometimes sling upstairs above pool table (pocket a few balls!)

Exit (Bar & Dance club)
Third floor, past the bar.

4 Men (Sex shop & Porn Cinema)
Behind the screen in upstairs cinema.

William Higgins' Le Salon
Back of shop.

Spijker (Bar)
Upstairs, past the pool table.

The Web (Bar)
Upstairs.

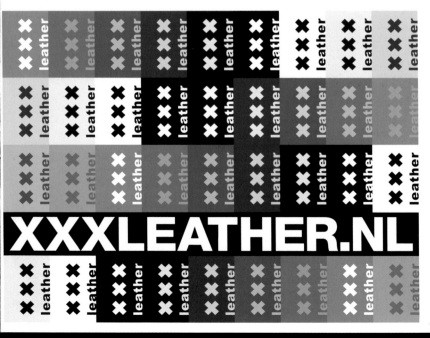

every 2nd & last sunday - shirtless & nude men only
Eagle, Warmoesstraat 90 - 4 till 8pm - € 7 - sex only safe

www.gala-amsterdam.nl - artwork: s. steeman

sex
on
sunday

Wild Side

www.wildside.dds.nl
Third Sat 8pm - 11pm
(except July and Aug)
Who: *Women only*
Wear: *Kinky & SM gear*
What ♫: *Varied*

A social and educational support group for all women with a personal interest in SM with other women, Wild Side hold great forums & get-togethers discussing various SM topics and techniques (whipping, sex toys, how to punish your partner's cat and deny her chocolate, etc). They hold monthly **SM workshops** (how is it only women know how to whip up a cosy flogging session?), SM beginners weekends annually (the perfect gift for the woman you thought had everything!) but their **SM Play Parties** are on hold till they find a new venue. They also publish a bilingual newsletter about every second month.

WALP
(Women at Leather Pride)

www.walp.dds.nl
Who: *Leatherwomen world-wide*
Wear: *Leather*
What ♫: *Networking & whip cracking*

Going strong since 1996, founders Tania and Denya once again confounded old-school feminists & titillated over 145 leatherwomen from all over the world with their 2006 international women's SM & Leather conference. It's stated primary aim is to *"create a social and educational network for leatherwomen within Europe and to encourage connections between leatherwomen in Europe and other continents."* But a quick peek at previous forum topics such as 'Art of Caning,' 'Tools for topping with love & emotions,' Japanese Rope Bondage workshops, a Slave Auction & SM party & demos in humiliation & degradation play makes one think that when these grrrls have fun they not only do it nastier but - considering their conference is spread over 10 fun-filled days - they also have more endurance than the gay leather boys who can only keep it up (the **Leather Pride** Festival) for 3 days! Check website for full details & updates.

Being truly Bent doesn't just mean being Gay or Lesbian. The great thing about Amsterdam's famed tolerance is that locals don't give a flying fuck whose genitals you play with, and respect your rights to do whatever you bloody well like with them. Consequently, there's a very healthy fetish scene for fetish folk of every sexual bent: from straight couples who like to dabble once a year, to serious swingers swapping wives more often than their kids do Pokemon cards.

Check out **www.fetishlights.nl** or **www.gofetish.nl** for full Holland-wide agenda of events.

The Clinic
Various venues
11pm – 5am
www.clinicweekend.com
Who: *Mostly straight; some gay boys*
Wear: *Fetish gear*
What ♪: *Varied*

These member-only parties are relatively intimate gatherings (max 500 people) made up of mostly straight 'swingers' with a few gay boys flirting with the bi-sex couples. To participate you have to be invited by a member and then apply for full membership once accepted.
Check website for updates on venues and other details.

Sameplace
Nassaukade 120 (Not on Map)
Mon - Sun 10pm - 3am
Fri/Sat til 4am
www.sameplace.nl
Who: *Sun 8pm: Straight couples (& a friend)*
Mondays 9pm - 1am Men only
Wear: *Whatever!*
What ♪: *varied*

"Freedom is the right not to lie about yourself." Sameplace sums up Amsterdam's famed sexual tolerance. An 'erotic café' & women-friendly meeting place it welcomes straight couples, gays, lesbians, cross dressers, transexuals, swingers & exhibitionists. There aren't any 'acts' or professionals on show, punters simply utilise the dance floor, stage or the *"several corners which provide some privacy."* When there's a "good atmosphere" the downstairs cellar is opened for invitees to enjoy the dark room, St Andrew's Cross & sling. Pushy women-unfriendly behaviour isn't tolerated (although pushy women, perversely, are encouraged).

Kinky Dreams
@ Lexion venue
Not on Map
10pm - 6am
www.kinkydreams.nl
Who: *Mainly Straight*
Wear: *Dress to impress - not yourself but the rest*
What ♪: *Varied*

A new player on the fetish scene, their first party a few years back got a decent turnout to a venue a long way out of town (and no shuttle buses), and most left satisfied (at least those not expecting a cab at 6am in way out Westzaan). Probably the least 'queer' of the mixed fetish parties, it (mostly) attracts the kind of crowd who get wet watching 3-ways that are about as exciting as Madonna, Britney & Christina's tongue-hockey *schtick*.

Wasteland

Various venues
Twice yearly
10pm till late
www.wasteland.nl

Who: *Men & Women, Homo & Hetero (but all of them very Bent!)*

Wear: *Leather, Uniforms, Plastic, Rubber, Metal, Cross-dress, Fetish, Glam and the decision of the door bitch is final!*

What ♫**:** *Hard Techno down-stairs, slightly more chilled & happier upstairs*

Full of incredibly sexy girls you wished you'd met when you naively thought all you needed was a really good bad girl (and their equally sexy boyfriends you wished you'd met when their E's were kicking in), Wasteland is one of those rare parties that demonstrates a straight crowd, given permission (and the right rubber outfits), can get just as bent as any group of gay men on GHB.

Like a VERY queer-friendly Heironymous Bosch painting with a throbbing techno beat, this fetish dance/sex party (self-proclaimed as Europe's largest) is held twice a year. While overwhelmingly hetero it also attracts a fairly large contingent of gay guys hovering around the single Hetero men high and horned up by hordes of rubberised French maids (so much so their website is often filled with complaints we're taking over. Funny, no-one seems to mind the bi-chicks giving each other lip reading lessons!). While a great place to witness the broadest display of human sexuality you could hope for (and quite a lot you wish you'd never seen up so close!) Wasteland's success and infamy also attracts packs of suburban pervs in rented PVC suits out for a walk on the wild side.

But where else cold you write eye-popping postcards home about:
• fabulous, ridiculous, horny and some VERY FUCKING SAD excuses for fetish outfits;
• black rubber hooded men with zippers for mouths being fed (both ends) from funnels
• actual proof some hetero guys DO eat pussy
• actual proof some gay guys don't mind the flavour of pussy (so long as it's sampled from the boyfriend's lap)
• dykes fisting on the dancefloor (and all you can think is 'Man, I hope she brought a nail file!')
• an old man in his 60s in army uniform asleep in the corner next to a pregnant dyke and her pals playing with the dick of a tattooed dwarf wielding a sabre (I'm not making this up, folks!)
• a lewd Louis XIV allowing his masterful Marie Antionette to dominate him with an assortment of strap-ons so alarming it seemed like Saddam's weapons of (m)ass destruction had finally been found. And, for her fevered finale, skilfully placed not one but TWO feet all the way inside her Bonaparte's butt (thankfully, after she'd kicked off the 9 inch stilettos!)

Being Amsterdam, cruising can take place just about *everywhere:* museums, shopping centres, cafes and in virtually every park, garden and square meter of turf with a bush big enough to blow someone behind. Beware though, many of the late night beats and cruising spots (*banen* in Dutch) - particularly in and around the Rose Garden in **Vondel Park** - are also often frequented by winsome young lads who aren't just groping your taut arse, but your bulging wallet and throbbing mobile phone as well. While discrete behaviour is generally tolerated by locals, various local councils (in response to complaints about used condoms found near children's areas) are trimming trees & undergrowth in efforts to discourage parks from becoming backrooms after dark, and fines for having sex in public view can be as high as €2,500. Police occasionally patrol at night but are more there to ensure safety than countering coupling in the copses. Remember: don't just cum & run, clean up around you as well as what's been left over you.

A great online resource for cruising and 'meeting places' for gay men (and that elusive breed: men-who-have-sex-with-other-men) is **www.banenoverzicht.net** for an incredibly extensive list of locations in and around Amsterdam.

Amsterdamse Bos
Where: *Amstelveen*
Who: *Men only*
When: *Day & Night*

Just a leisurely 20 minute bike ride from Leidseplein and you're in the 'satellite town' of Amstelveen & a great nature & recreational area of woodland walks, horse trails, lakes, swimming pools & offically sanctioned nude beaches. Accordingly, there's LOTS of cruising & action in various parking spots after dark.

Bijlmerpark
Where: *Corner of Gooiseweg & A9. Park Kelbergen, walk under Gooseweg & take path thru bushes*
Who: *Men only; diverse*
When: *Day & Night*

The Bijlmer Housing projects are home to a poorer, ethnic community, so while the men here are more racially diverse than the predominantly white inner-city parks, there's always the potential here for less tolerance & more danger for lone walkers after dark. After recent tree pruning it's less busy but due to the nearby A9 freeway it can get busy around rush hour (5pm to 7pm). Summer is the best time to sample the darker meat on offer but the first week in July is the local Kwakoe Festival where overt cruising isn't advised.

Erasmuspark
Where: *Jan Van Galenstraat*
Who: *Men only*
When: *Night*

Named after a Dutch classical scholar this park has bushes, a toilet block and plenty of potential passing trade - you do the math!

Gaasperplas

Where: *A9 exit to Weesp*
Who: *Men only*
When: *Day & Night*

When the weather's willing this quiet spot for strolling through the sand dunes can prove fruitful. Recent controls by locals have forced activities back into the bushes but in summer the action continues all day & well into the night.

Nieuwe Meer

Where: *Oude Haagseweg - Lake near Schiphol Airport*
Who: *Men only*
When: *Day & Night*
Also check out: http://groups. msn.com/denieuwemeer

The Nieuwe Meer (or *De Oeverlanden* as the banks of the lake are more accurately, but rarely called) out toward Schiphol Airport may seem WAY out of town but it's a great spot for nature lovers who enjoy running into large, hairy beasts at every turn. In fact, many are hung like bulls because, well, they are bulls. In a rather quaint effort to (apparently) combat the growth of weeds (and discourage the growth of other queer wildlife in the undergrowth) the local council has installed a small group of Scottish Highlanders (alas, not a patrol of men in kilts, but long-horned cattle). But don't worry, these shaggy, incredibly docile animals add a certain bucolic charm - although hiking handballers should perhaps be wary of waving their red hankies about.

In summer, this place is the busiest beat this side of the Falluja Police force & really jumps, and can even get busy in winter (though with fewer exposed body parts) and because of its popularity, is relatively safe (although on hot days when it's crawling with cruisers it could do with a little more isolation). Nieuwe Meer is difficult to get to without a car, as it's a good 40 minute bike ride from the centre of Amsterdam. But, if you like the wind in your hair while some stranger's hands grab both ears, it can be well worth the trip. Take buses 44, 180 or 181 and get off near the Mexx & IBM office complexes on Johan Huizingalaan. Walk under the freeway flyover and along the bike path until you cross a small bridge. The main path forks to the left and the right circumnavigating the park, or head straight through the small gate and follow the meandering dirt trail through the bushes (if you're in need of a milking).

Oosterpark

Where: *Trams 3, 7 & 9*
Who: *Men only*
When: *Mainly night*

Summer evenings & weekends this park can get reasonably busy with a very mixed crowd (blacks, moroccans, rent boys, old, students & tourists) as well as hetero locals letting their dogs sniff a few butts too. Most action is by the skate ring, pond and bridge. Occasional police patrols - sometimes with torches (luckily not flaming).

Sarphatipark

Where: *De Pijp*
Who: *Men only*
When: *Mainly night*

This charming park, located in the middle of the funky *de Pijp* neighbourhood, can get so busy some summer evenings that there's still cocks a-showing by the time the Cock's a-crowing. Due to it's small size there's not a lot of space for privacy so expect more group action on offer - mostly near the basketball courts on the eastern side. Police 'safety' patrols aren't uncommon and, as it's a busy children's park during the day, be discrete & dispose of used condoms appropriately.

Sloterpark

Where: *President Allendelaan*
Who: *Men only*
When: *Mainly night*

Given the good amount of gay boys who congregate at the nearby **Sloterparkbad** swimming pool this sprawling lakeside park should see some action - but we've yet to hear any details. Still, if we build it (the rumour) will you cum?

Vliegenbos

Where: *Amsterdam Noord*
Who: *Men only*
When: *Day & Night*

Despite the near-by student camp site in summer, this moderately busy park across the IJ Harbour in North Amsterdam is also known for it's other 'camping ground' that attracts a more older 'patron' to the delights on offer behind the trees near the pond. Discretion advised.

Vondelpark

Where: *Rose garden – south of the lake*
Who: *Men only*
When: *Day & Night*

The Rose Garden attracts more than just bees and in the summer months there are plenty of gay boys lying around in speedos, scattered about the flower beds checking out each other's arrangements. After dark in the summer months is often busy but definitely at your own risk as there's pricks to be found not only on the roses.

Westerpark

Where: *Haarlemmerweg*
Who: *Men only*
When: *Day & Night*

Recently renovated & extended into the *Westergasfabriek* (a former gas works) this always busy park rewards a visit day or night. Pay special attention to the single-minded organisms around the pond in the older section, and fuzzy balls can often be found behind the tennis courts. Mostly safe, but keep an eye out for youths stumbling through on their way home from the clubs.

Zandvoort aan Zee

Where: *Far South end of the beach & dunes*
Who: *Men only*
When: *Day & early evening*

The train from Centraal Station to Zandvoort takes about 30 minutes (most times with a change in Haarlem), and the walk to the gay end of this enormously long beach is about the same, so make sure you bring a bottle of water. From the Station keep walking until you find the beach, turn left and when you've reached the nudist end you know you're getting warmer (weather dependant!). Once you see more disco tits than actual women's breasts frying in the sun you'll know you've finally hit the gay beach.

Hustler Bars & Houses with Boys

Just off the top end of Rembrandtplein runs the narrow Paardenstraat (literally: street of horses) where young Arabic & Romanian colts can be hired for a quick ride around the block. The boys for rent here tend to loiter in the alley or (when it's colder) hang out in **Music Box**. The quaint Dutch term 'Houses with Boys' pretty much means a brothel where punters sit at a bar 'socialising' with the boys before deciding who to continue with further in a more private room.

Those looking for trannies for rent can head to the Red Light District, in particular the small lanes around Bloedstraat connecting the Nieuwmarkt to the Oudezijds Achterburgwal, where the 'girls' ply their trade behind the famous windows.

The closing of the upstairs/downstairs venues **Blue Boy** and **Why Not** bars illustrates changes within Europe. With the US dollar's slide against the Euro the older gay chicken hawks who used to frequent this infamous House of Boys for its live & private shows have now flown the coop forcheaper finger-lickin' fun in far-off Eastern Europe.

Boys Club 21

Map 7, p.24
Spuistraat 21
+31 20 622 8828
Open from 1 till 1
(Fri Sat till 2)

Walking into Amsterdam's last surviving House of Boys is like entering some bizarro alternative universe where the gay pecking order is turned upside down. Here, cute young things compete for the attention (and more importantly, the wallets) of mostly elderly balding men with paunches. So if you're somewhat past your prime you can sit at the bar and drink in all the attention. For €120 you get to choose not only the boy you'd like, but also the theme of the room in which to get to know him a whole lot better (well, as much intercourse as you can physically squeeze into an hour).

The Music Box

Map 35, p.15
Paardenstraat 10
+31 20 620 4110
Wednesday, Thursday, Sunday
9pm – 3am
Fri/Sat 9pm – 4am

Despite the rather cool disdain from the rent boys who clump together socialising when not working, The Music Box is pretty much a standard traditional Dutch pub with a surprisingly pleasant and friendly ambience. You'll soon work out who's who as the crowd can be easily distinguished between those with bulging wallets and those willing to relieve them. Catch the eye of your favourite boy and he'll soon be sidling up asking for you to buy him a drink. What transpires after that is up to you. As such, anyone dealing with those from the 'oldest profession' should make sure they keep their wits (and personal possessions) about them.

*NOTE: A recent Police raid resulted in the arrest of 20 young East European boys for lacking proper work permits. While taking a passport into such venues isn't advised, thanks to our current conservative (some might say xenophobic) Government's policies, if you're not carrying any form of I.D. you'll also be fined (and probably not flattered to be suspected of being a refugee rent boy).

Massage & Male Escorts

Call Boys
+31 20 679 5098
11am till 5am

A variety of boys on call, specialising in SM, Leather & Black preferences. Reliable and discrete. Rates from €145 per hour; higher for 'speciality' requests.

City Boys
+31 20 400 4455
2pm till 6am

Services only the inner city and Schiphol surrounds. Rates from €135 per hour.

Homo Escort
+31 20 662 3142
11am till 5am

More than a few hard ons on homo escorts are owned by hard up hetero boys. But these boys are all gay - all the time! Rates from €135 per hour.

People Male Escorts
+31 20 662 9990
24 hour service
www.peoplemale.com

Unlike a lot of other fly-by-night establishments these guys have been around for years and know the value of providing good honest service. Reputable & carefully selected boys of every type. Rates from €145 per hour.

Michael's Boys Escorts
+31 20 618 1824
www.michaelsboysescorts.com

Mediating the escort services of 'fine young men' (aged 18-35) this gay-owned business offers a good level of quality and service. Rates start from €140 for an hourly escort.

*Note:

Ads for individual escorts and 'erotic' masseurs can also be found in the back pages of **Gay News** and **Gay & Night**.

Thermos Day

Map 77, p.35
Raamstraat 33
+31 20 623 9158
Daily - Noon till 11pm
Sat & holidays Noon till 10pm
Sundays 11am till 10pm
Entrance €18
(under 23yr olds €13.50)
www.thermos.nl

Who: *Men only*

Wear: *Little towels artfully tied to conceal as much as they reveal*

What ♪: *Chilled music with occasional groaning*

Holland's less than tropical weather often means spending time indoors where it's warm and dry. But no visit is complete without spending at least one day warm and wet in the five floors of luxury of Amsterdam's premier sauna (and self-proclaimed "largest in Europe"). Including steam room, dry sauna, roof terrace, restaurant, video room, bar and swimming pool Thermos is spacious, clean and often very busy, rightly earning the reputation as one of the best saunas in the world.

SPECIAL EVENTS:
Steam After Parties - 5am till 10am, roughly once a month, check www.amsterdam4gays.com for party dates.
Bear Baths - First Saturday of the month, 2 pm - 10 pm

Thermos Night

Map 71, p.35
Kerkstraat 58-60
+31 20 623 4936
Nightly 11pm till 8am
Saturday till 10am
Entrance €18
www.thermos.nl

Who: *Men only*

Not as large and sumptuous as the day sauna, but uses pretty much the same successful formula: "If you clean it, they will cum!" Gets busy late when the pubs and clubs close around 3 or 4 in the morning with hot young things wanting to soak their tired feet (or just wear them as earrings).

Boomerang

Map 23, p.24
Heintjehoeksteeg 8
+31 20 622 6162
Daily 9am till 11pm
Entrance €13,50
(Under 24: € 11.50)

Who: *Men only*

This compact sauna in the red light district is certainly not everyone's cup of tea. Being small it does have an intimate atmosphere that is sometimes lacking in larger 'meat factories'. Still advertising itself as 'new', despite the fact that the sauna has been open for more than 8 years, it is starting to look a little shabby around the edges.

Sauna Damrak

Not on Map
Damrak 54
+31 20 622 6012
Mon to Fri 10am – 11pm
Sat/Sunday Noon till 8pm

Who: *Men only; Monday to Friday. Mixed - Weekends*

This place hasn't quite made up its mind if it's a gay sauna or not. There are no cabins, but still plenty of action in the steam room and spa. Still sporting its original seventies interior (so its now oddly fashionable) this rather queer place is, at least, centrally located.

Get your chill & thrill

THERMOS
SAUNA
AMSTERDAM

Thermos Day Sauna
Raamstraat 33, Amsterdam
Open: daily from noon till 11 p.m.
Saturday and holidays from noon till 10 p.m.
Sunday from 11 a.m. till 10 p.m.

Thermos Night Sauna
Kerkstraat 58-60, Amsterdam
Open: daily from 11 p.m. till 8 a.m.

Sex shops & Cinemas

Adonis
Map 13, p.24
Warmoesstraat 92
10am till 1am
weekends till 3am
http://adonis-4men.info/

Slightly dilapidated DVD, video and bookshop with large cinema at the back. Busy, lots of action going on behind the movie screen.

Alfa Blue
Map 3, p.24
Nieuwendijk 26
Daily 9am till Midnight

DVDs, toys and magazines. Left side hetero porn, right side gay porn in this clean and smart little sex shop next to Le Salon. There are cabins at the back showing gay and straight porn flicks.

B1 Cinema
Map 44c, p.15
Regulierbreestraat 4
Daily 9am till Midnight
Sunday noon till midnight
www.b1sex.nl

Busy 3 level porn palace showing straight stick flicks on the 1st floor and gay stuff above (with quite a few guys unafraid to get in literally over their heads braving the stairs in between). A few private cabins with glory holes and a blacker backroom than Calcutta.

Bronx
Map 70, p.35
Kerkstraat 53-55
Daily Noon till Midnight
www.bronx.nl

DVDs, magazines, toys, gifts and clothes in this newly refurbished gay store. As well a small lounge to browse the free mags, three internet terminals, coffee and cruise cabins (€9.50 entrance) downstairs. It looks so spacious and comfortable that you almost want to move in.

Drakes
Map 11, p.24
Damrak 61
Daily 9am till midnight
www.drakes.nl

Looking like a regular tourist shop from the Damrak, up back lies an impressive range of porn videos, DVDs, magazines & sex toys. Recently renovated throughout, the workers seem to have overlooked a number of conveniently placed 'ventilation holes' upstairs in the cruisy video cabins. Busy during lunch & after work.

4 Men
Map 7, p.24
Spuistraat 21
Daily 11am till 1am
http://adonis-4men.info

Tiny cinema and video rooms but as it's been renovated this century it's considerably cleaner than many of its competitors .

Miranda Sex Shop
Map 44b, p.15
Reguliersbreestraat 7
Daily 10am till Midnight

Sex shop with two cinemas upstairs - one gay, one straight. Plenty of boys happy to sit both sides of the aisle here.

William Higgins' Le Salon
Map 2, p.24
Nieuwendijk 20-22
Daily 10am till Midnight

A split-level labyrinth, including about ten cabins with glory holes showing non-stop porn and a small cinema all at the back of this well stocked porn shop. €10 will get you an all-day pass.

SLEEP

Remember when BB just meant a cheap bedsit where you got a bread roll and a cup of coffee in the morning (and had nothing to do with whether you wore a condom or not)? Remember when 'gay-friendly' meant the front desk discretely offering you a queen-sized bed? Well, being Amsterdam you never have to worry about keeping a 'low profile' as virtually every hotel in town is 'gay and lesbian friendly.' As long as you don't frighten the other guests with your fetish gear and hooded gimps coming and going on all fours at all hours, they won't care who you sleep with (besides, it's against Dutch law to refuse patrons on the grounds of sexuality).

But if you *are* looking for a place to wear your harness while eating your morning hash browns, then check out the gay men and lesbian only listings below. Our 'queer friendly' list refers to predominantly gay-owned or queer guest list venues but may not (necessarily) be exclusively Homo. So try not to throw *too* big a hissy fit if there are smaller guests playing with dolls more loudly than you are.

Amsterdam 37

Gay Centre Spot
Map 75a, p.35
Prinsengracht 430
+31 20 625 6748 (Annemarie)
borsboom.a@tiscali.nl
Double room with own bath,
sauna & kitchenette €95 for
two people per night

(see: Sleep – Queer Friendly Hotels)

Centrally located on the beautiful Prinsengracht and not far from Leidseplein, this place is more like staying with a distant Dutch Aunt than strict B&B accommodation. However, it's NOT strictly a women's only venue. But with only one room on offer, the 'garden suite', it's strictly what you want it to be (although those over 1.85 meters tall may feel a little cramped by the 17th century beamed ceilings). Discounts for long term arrangements. Canoes also available for guests!

Freeland Hotel

(see: Queer Friendly Hotels)

The Golden Bear

(see: Gay Only Hotels)

Johanna's
Not on Map
Van Hogendorpplein 62
+31 20 684 8596
Mobile: +31 (0)6 413 3056
http://home.planet.
nl/~johanna6/
Rooms from €90 for two
people per night.

Johanna's is a small 'home-stay style' B&B with just 2 bedrooms that's situated in the artsy Westergasfabriek (old Gas Factory) district about 15 minutes walk from Centraal Station. Like the Gay Centre Spot it's a place for women, but gay men are also welcome. Cosy with shared bathroom and toilet facilities. Non smoking and be prepared to share with an aging cat and an (at times) eccentric host!

Liliane's Home
Not on Map
Sarphatistraat 119
+31 20 627 4006
Single room €50 - €85
Double room €80 - €100
Breakfast and all taxes included
in room rate

This rather upmarket *Herenhuis* (Dutch for Gentleman's House) doesn't, in fact allow any type of man (gentle or otherwsie) to stay and is the sole, exclusively women's only accomodation in all of Amsterdam (although she has been known to make an exception admitting nice gay boys for Queen's Day and New Year's Eve), offering 7 rooms (2 with private bathroom). No children and no pets.

Anco Hotel

Map 28, p.24
Oudezijds Voorburgwal 55
+31 20 624 1126
www.ancohotel.nl
Dorms €43
Single room €65
Double room €90

The Anco Hotel is a living legend in the Amsterdam leather scene, just a few blocks away from the infamous Warmoesstraat bars. Exclusively gay men, mostly leather & skins. The small downstairs bar is open to the public and can get (on occasion) a few hotel patrons working up a bit of Dutch courage before braving the busloads of drunk football tourists trawling the streets of the nearby Red Light District. Continental breakfast included in prices.

Black Tulip

Map 19, p.24
Geldersekade 16
+31 20 427 0933
www.blacktulip.nl
Single room €115
Standard Double €145
Deluxe Double room €170
Front Fantasy room €195
inclusive of local taxes &
breakfast buffet

Beautiful and classy 16th Century leather hotel, minutes away from Centraal Station and leather bars. All rooms have an impressive combination of luxury and lust with private bathroom (some with whirlpool) as well as sling, bondage hooks and other beautifully crafted equipment such as St Andrew's cross, bondage chair, stocks or metal cage. The Special Fantasy Room comes with extra large gimp… er, 'guestroom' and even more 'fun' equipment (the mind boggles!).

Flatmates

Map 82, p.35
+31 20 620 1545
www.flatmates.nl

Check their site to find a whole range of beautiful apartments, studios, B&Bs and house boats to rent throughout the city.

Ebab

www.ebab.com
From €30 single
Map 30, p.14
Map 31, p.15
Map 1, p.27
Maps 76, 88 p.35

If you're on a tight budget or just want to meet some locals, this is a great site to check out. Ebab (enjoy bed and breakfast) arranges rooms in private homo homes throughout the world, with a good selection here in Amsterdam. You can often also rent the whole apartment.

The Golden Bear

Map 67, p.35
Kerkstraat 37
+31 20 624 4785
www.goldenbear.nl
Single room from €62 - 101
Double room from €76 - 116

Amsterdam's first exclusively gay hotel since 1948. Situated in two historic buildings dating from 1737 close to gay bars and saunas. Leather and (naturally!) bear friendly, mostly gay men stay here, but the hotel also happily welcomes lesbians. Breakfast included.

Stablemaster Bar and Hotel

Map 21, p.24
Warmoesstraat 23
+31 20 625 0148
www.stablemaster.nl
Single room €65, Double room €95

Small hotel in the middle of the leather & Red Light District. Famous for its Jack Off parties **(see: Fuck - Men Only Parties)**. Thankfully, with separate entrance (so no greasy doorknobs to deal with). The bar downstairs opens Thursday to Monday 9pm to 1am (Friday & Saturday until 2am) - so pack your earplugs!

Adriaen van Ostade B&B

Map 86, p.35
+31 (0) 6 5338 4723
www.amsterdambedbreakfast.com

Two large, sunny and quiet rooms in this new B&B situated in the trendy De Pijp neighbourhood. Close to Albert Cuyp market and the many restaurants and cafes in the area, and walking distance to the centre of town.

Amistad

Map 72, p.35
Kerkstraat 42
+31 20 624 8074
www.amistad.nl
Standard Single €75
Standard Double €94
Single Deluxe €115
Double Deluxe €150

One way to tell a truly gay hotel is that they serve breakfast from the wonderfully civilised hours of 10am till 2pm. One of the oldest gay hotels in Amsterdam (formerly known as the West End Hotel but now fully renovated), this (mostly gay) designer hotel offers a smart, stylish and friendly place to relax in sexy tones of red and *'Breakfast at Tiffany's'* murals. ***Note:** Internet lounge available for €2.50/hour.

Amsterdam 37

Not on Map
Beursstraat 37
+31 20 620 24 03
www.amsterdam37.com
From €190 (including breakfast or lunch, snacks, beverages and all taxes & fees)

These private apartments and suites have a kind of dual personality. Impressively catered sleeping, kitchen and dining facilities (filled with goodies like snacks, drinks and plenty of fresh towels) are right next door to even more impressively goody-filled dungeon playrooms. But here's the best bit: they don't give a damn who you may want to beat up, train to go bow wow or just cook a good bowl of spag bol for. Whether you're L,B,G,T or Hetero (or just want to sit in your cage until you're told what you are), all are welcome. You even get to choose erotic art, with or without penises, to decorate your place!

Barangay B&B

Map 2a, p.24
Droogbak 15a
+31 (0)6 250 45432 (mobile)
www.barangay.nl
Rooms from €80 (low) to
€ 130 (high)
(Includes breakfast)

'Barangay' is Filipino for "small village" and inside this typical narrow Dutch canal house you're transported back to the era of Dutch Colonial rule with "tropical accent" decorations of rattan, bamboo and mosquito netting over 4 poster beds. Built in 1777 this cute B&B is just a short stroll to Centraal Station. All rooms are non-smoking but there are 2 rooms that connect onto a small patio where smoking is permitted.

Cake Under My Pillow

Map 86a, p.35
Ferdinand Bolstraat 10
+31 20 751 0936
www.cakeundermypillow.com
Rooms from €90 to €160

(see also: Eat – Taart Van Mijn Tante)
Those on a diet should stay well clear of this cute lil B&B in the funky *de Pijp* area. Not only is it just around the corner from the famed Heineken Museum & brewery, but you're literally sleeping above some of Amsterdam's most mouth watering cakes. Owners Sieman & Noam (from Taart Van Mijn Tante below) have fully renovated this 19th century former merchant's building to provide charming & comfy rooms with king-sized beds (some with ensuites, others share a bathroom across the hall). Close to a great array of cool eateries & funky bars & walking distance to the major museums.

Centre Apartments Amsterdam

Map 22, p.24
Heintje Hoeksteeg
+31 20 627 2503
http://centre-apartments-amster-dam.nl
Studios €125, apartments €125
Apartments €110 to €145

Gerard and Chris provide private self-catering apartments and studios just around the corner from Warmoesstraat and Centraal Station. No pets, children or use of Crisco or Eros lubricants (we take it they don't just mean using all of these things combined!)
Minimum 3 night stay required.

Chico's Guesthouse

Not on Map
Sint Willibrordusstraat 77H
+31 20 675 4241
Double rooms (private bath-room) from €70

Located in the funky part of Amsterdam called *de Pijp* is this cosy 4 room mixed guesthouse. Great location for soaking up a non-touristy side of Amsterdam with great cafes, restaurants and the city's best street market Albert Cuyp nearby.

The Eel House

Not on Map
2nd Lindendwarsstraat 21
+31 20 330 0544
http://eelhouse.nl/
Double rooms €90 (low),
€120 (high season)

Named after the quaint Dutch tradition of tying a greased eel to a rope suspended above a canal and having contestants try to jump from a boat for the slippery prize (thankfully, for the eel now banned), you might think this place is for serious kink fetishists only. But in reality this small but charming 17th century gable-roofed guesthouse nestled in the historic Jordaan area of Amsterdam oozes luxury & comfort. And it's the attention to the gayest of details that'll make you feel at home: two sunny and modern rooms, each with microwave, mini fridge & dishes, queen-sized bed, bath and balcony, fresh flowers on arrival, free coffee, tea, mineral water, wine, fruit & chocolates for the duration of your stay, plus 6 fresh towels daily for the cleanliness freaks (and not a greasy eel in sight!).

Freeland Hotel

Map 80, p.35
Marnixstraat 386
1017 PL Amsterdam
+31 20 622 7511
www.hotelfreeland.com
Single €65, Double €110

Pascale and Rik welcome you to their very friendly hotel with a great location on the corner of the Leidseplein offering you "real Dutch open-mindedness and a feel-good ambience". 15 clean rooms, free internet access in the lobby and free WIFI, a welcome cup of coffee and walking distance to the main cultural attractions, not to mention the gay bars. Also especially welcomes dykes. Includes full Dutch breakfast.

Friendship B&B

Not on Map
Achtergracht 17G
+31 20 622 1294
www.friendshipbnb.nl
Entire Houseboat €110 for 2 people or €300 for 3 nights. Discounts for longer stays. Use of extra bedroom: add €15 per person (2 max)

If you're coming to the 'Venice of the North' why not stay on a houseboat and get a real feel for the aquatic Amsterdam life? The Friendship B&B (get it, Friend *Ship*!) is a fully-equipped & comfortable houseboat on a quiet but central canal with 2 double bedrooms, kitchen/living area & bath and shower. Owner Timos retains a separate part of the houseboat as his office during weekday afternoons (usually between 2 and 6 pm) and is happy to offer assistance or advice. Two bicycles and use of the on-board computer are also available free of charge!

Hotel NL

Map 78, p.35
Nassaukade 368
+31 20 689 0030
www.nl-hotel.com
Single room from €85 - 200
Double room from €110 - 200

This beautiful new designer hotel near Leidseplein was recently voted by *Het Parool*, (the main Amsterdam newspaper), as the best small hotel in the city. With elegance, an attention to colours and details and a 'zen-like tranquil Dutch touch' ambience, if you're a design queen this is where you'll want to stay.

ITC

Map 91, p.15
Prinsengracht 1051
+31 20 623 0230
www.itc-hotel.com
Single €59-95
Double €89-135
Triple €109-165

Very cute little (mostly gay & lesbian) hotel in a traditional 18th century canal house overlooking the stunning Prinsengracht. A great part of town for wandering, the Hotel is just around the corner from Rembrandtplein and the funky Utrechtsestraat with cosy cafes, good restaurants and one of Amsterdam's best music shops Concerto, and only a short stroll to the gay & lesbian venues. 24 hour free gay TV channels.

Lloyd Hotel and Cultural Embassy

Not on Map
Oostelijke Handelskade 34
+31 20 561 3636
www.lloydhotel.com
Rooms from €95 to €450

In the newly developed eastern harbour is this great design hotel which offers rooms from one to five stars (from shared bathroom to a room based around a gigantic bath and a bed for eight!). The 'cultural embassy' organises exhibitions and gives guests a full run-down on what's going on in town.

Maes B&B

Map 1d, p.26
Herenstraat 26
+31 20 427 5165
www.bedandbreakfastamsterdam.com
Apartment from €115
Apartments (max 4 people) from €135

Named after Nicolaas Maes, a famous 17th century Dutch painter, this cosy and friendly private house dates from 18th century but has been lovingly renovated. Offering two double rooms (with king sized beds!) the B&B is located in a quiet residential street between Herengracht & Keizersgracht and just around the corner from Anne Frank House and the Homomonument. Non smoking rooms.

Radio Inn Hostel

Map 92, p.35
Utrechtsedwarstraat79
+ 31 20 625 0345
www.radioinn.nl
€35 per bed per night

The only hostel that advertises specifically to gays, lesbians and bisexuals, there's sure to be plenty of fun and games in these 2, 3, 4 or even 5 bed dorm-rooms (and hissy fits for the shared bathrooms) in this great part of town. Also pet and straight friendly.

Sunhead of 1617

Map 57b, p.26
Herengracht 152
+31 20 626 1809
www.sunhead.com
Rooms from €99 - 139

Named after the ornate moulded sun stone on the façade of one of Amsterdam's oldest listed canal houses. This small and friendly "gay owned and very straight friendly" B&B offers value for money and great character. High vaulted ceilings and exposed beams in spacious rooms containing fridge, microwave, tea/coffee facilities & TV.

Triple Five Guesthouse

Map 66, p.26
Prinsengracht 555
+31 20 428 3809
www.triplefive.nl
Rooms from €95 – €135

Centrally located, between Anne Frank House and Leidseplein on the beautiful Prinsengracht canal, Triple Five is within walking distance to just about everything in town. Beautifully renovated luxury bedrooms with private bathrooms as well as a fully-equipped apartment for 4+ guests available.

Truelove

Map 1b, p.26
Prinsenstraat 4
+31 20 320 2500
www.truelove.be
Double room from €75
Suite from €110

Antiques and Art in the basement and groundfloor, with a cute guesthouse on the 3 floors above (each artfully decorated room has coffee, tea, mineral water and wine!). What more could an old queen ask for? Minimum stay of 2 nights on weekends. Non smoking. Also, apartments available on the Prinsengracht.

There's a LOT more to Amsterdam than just the gay ghettos, coffeeshops and Red Light District. The city really is rich in history and culture (fuck, I sound like one of those dreadful CNN travel advertorials!). Like the **Homomonument** itself, our many gay and lesbian communities are so well integrated into the fabric of the city that they can be easily overlooked. Yet our queer presence is an important and fundamental element of Dutch society. Take a tour, sit in on a discussion forum or just enjoy one of the many gay and lesbian events held throughout the year. Just make sure you learn more than where the best backrooms are.

Koninginnedag (Queen's Birthday)
April 30th, entire city

Although Queen Beatrix's actual birthday is earlier in the year, she's kept the date set by her mother Juliana to celebrate when the weather is (generally) kinder to outdoor drinking. The entire city is taken over by the quaint Dutch tradition of selling every imaginable piece of crap on the streets (the children's market in Vondelpark being the cutest if not the quietest with every little rug rat out busking with toy pianos, violins, accordians & bloody recorders), beer stands on every corner (although since the near-riots a few years back this has changed slightly) and the annual pissing-in-the-canal festival by the hordes that pack the narrow streets tighter (& smellier!) than a pickled herring tin.

Gay parties are held along the **Amstel**, **Halvemaansteeg**, **Reguliersdwarsstraat** and at the **Homomonument** (see: Roze Wester Festival below). A few years back the City Council - in a somewhat naive hope of calming down the drinking binges & subsequent mayhem - decided to once again allow Koninginnenacht (Queen's Day Eve) for everyone to blow off steam the night before and (hopefully) be quietly nursing hangovers on the actual day of the Royal festivities. As if!

Roze Wester Festival
Homomonument
www.gala-amsterdam.nl
April 29 & 30

In honour of Beatrix's always formidable frocks & hats worthy of an architecture award, Queen's Night 2005 saw the inaugural (and ruthless!) **Drag Queen Olympics**. Events range from high heel sprints to sashay marathons & hand bag tossing competitions, ending in the inevitable synchronised hissy fit/falling in the gutter/pissed to the gills demonstration sports, staged well into the wee hours. 7pm til midnight.

On Queen's Day the **Homomonument** forms the backdrop to a festival of music, performances & DJs. Noon til 9pm.

Remembrance Day
May 4th, 7:30pm till 8:30pm

On Remembrance Day at 8pm, along with other commemorations to the war dead held throughout the country, **COC Amsterdam** hold a solemn two-minute silence at the **Homomonument**, followed by speeches (in Dutch) by local dignitaries and the laying of elaborate wreaths on the triangle leading down into the Keizersgracht.

Liberation Day
May 5th

Throughout the Netherlands this day is the celebration of the end of World War II. The **Homomonument** is the site of the only homo event on this day. As well as hosting a gay and lesbian fair, with stalls from around 30 local queer groups, there's stage performances throughout the day, closing with a giant outdoor dance party (until 11pm). Run on a non-commercial basis, this event still manages to pull some of the best DJs around and funkiest crowds in town. Always draws lots of dykes as well.

AIDS Memorial Day
June - Dominicuskerk, Spuistraat 12
www.hivnet.org

2007 witnessed the 25th anniversary memorial to our community's continued loss. A moving multi-religious ceremony at the Dominicus church including readings, naming of deceased family & friends, lighting candles for each of the continents, culminating in the traditional singing of *'The Rose'* (seriously) and the release of hundreds of white balloons above the canals.

Dutch Transgender Film Festival
May - Cinema de Balie
www.transgenderfilmfestival.com

A bi-annual festival of films, discussions, performances & exhibitions as well as parties are all part of this non-profit group's plans to encourage visibilty and positive representation of transgender issues.

Mr Gay Netherlands
April

This annual cross between a beauty pageant and an under-done chicken raffle sees Holland's 'finest' boys strut the stage competing in such manly categories as Mr Swimwear and Mr Congeniality that makes the climatic scene of *'Little Miss Sunshine'* look like a Mr Universe championship by comparison. Like watching kittens in a car crash it's kinda cute but painful, as well being hilarious, tacky and, sometimes, surprisingly sexy as the boys take it all a bit too seriously battling to represent Holland at the Mr Gay Europe awards later in the year. Definitely worth checking out if you're in town during the contest but don't let the 'Mr' title fool you: these over-excited, barely pubescent Mama's boys should really be in a Master Bates competition instead.

(We Are) Amsterdam Pride
First weekend in August - entire city
www.amsterdampride.nl

After more than 10 years of bickering, backstabbing, bitching and just bad brinkmanship the Amsterdam City Council (not at all proud of organisers Gay Business Association's petty squabbles - but who, it must be said, built the event from scratch in '98 into one of the world's great gay prides) finally broke the monopoly on the event after GBA foolishly threatened to take their bat and ball home rather than share their pride and joy with other (non GBA) gay boys and girls wanting to play. So, it was up to new organisers Pro Gay to cobble together a somewhat lacklustre (but admittedly last-minute) 2006 canal parade. Then in 2007, Pro Gay unveiled the highly inventive rebranding We Are Amsterdam Pride (a name only a very large committee could love) and mentioned they'd be sharing the organising duties with the GBA after all. How this turns out is anyone's guess (but don't expect this cruise to be smooth sailing!)

However, They Who Are Amsterdam Pride have promised an extended festival week of gay and lesbian celebrations (an improvement from the meagre few days of previous events); from open air film screenings, sports competitions and church services to parties for virtually every queer community scattered across town. On the nights before and after the parade, street parties are held at **Halve Maansteeg**, the **Amstel** and **Rembrandtplein** (for trad Dutch fare), **Reguliersdwarsstraat** (young & trendy), **Paardenstraat** (women), the **Warmoesstraat** (leather), as well as a great all-types party at the **Homomonument** for those who prefer not to be pigeon-holed. Mega-crowded dance parties are thrown by all the usual suspects (as well as plenty of sharks fishing for fags by fluttering rainbow flags for only a few days) so check out www.amsterdam4gays.com for the full agenda and guide to the best gigs about town, or stop by **Pink Point** for more details.

The highlight of the festival is Saturday's colourful canal parade held on the Prinsengracht with around 100 oh-so-gaily-decorated boats and other floating fantasies watched by a genuinely adoring crowd of approximately 250,000 - if the weather holds (so grab those prime bridge-top viewing spots early folks!)

Summer Camp
August - Amsterdam Pride Weekend
www.gala-amsterdam.nl

A four day queer open air festival held at the **Homomonument** run by non-profit group **GALA** with DJs, drag performances, music, fashion, dancing, circus acts, friendship lounge & food stalls from Thursday to Sunday during **Amsterdam Pride** weekend. Tapping into Amsterdam's reserves of creative talents GALA often works in co-operation with groups & venues like **Art Launch** and **The Sugar Factory**.

Hartjesdag
3rd weekend in August, Zeedijk

Legend has it that since the middle ages, the 3rd weekend of August was a time for local folk to put on a frock or wig and parade around town as members of the opposite sex. The tradition was stopped by the occupying Nazis during WWII (the ultimate gate-crashing party-poopers), it was recently revived in 1997. The narrow **Zeedijk** gets packed all weekend with onlookers and DIY dragsters jostling for position. Sunday afternoon, when the boldest Drag Queens and Kings parade around the **Nieuwmarkt**, is a highlight along with the voting for the Ms Zeedijk Best Drag at the **Queen's Head**. Watch out for **Pink Point's** own (very sexy) Jennifer Hopelezz - J. Ho's fake butt's been prone to fly out during routines!

Leather Pride
Last week in October/First week in November, www.leatherpride.nl

Amsterdam's reputation as a Gay Capital has been built (largely) upon a leathery image. So sadly, when compared to other festivals like San Francisco's Folsom Street and Dore Alley or Chicago's IML, our festival is, in fact, so light on it could be called *Leatherette Pride* - it looks like the real thing, only cheaper! But while the **Playgrounds** parties may be a crafty marketing campaign by local leather outfitters to sell more twisted gear to tourists, these huge warehouse/fetish parties are still one of the biggest gigs in Europe for many rough and tumble tykes with enormous playrooms, watersports areas and dark mazes alongside an always pumping dancefloor. Leather Pride organisers however, could do worse than taking a leathery leaf from the **Women At Leather Pride's** own bi-annual sister act for tips on how to stage a truly impressive 10 day festival of forums, workshops, dances, sex-fests and education alongside the every-day depravity. And, in fact, it seems the criticism is (finally!) sinking through the organiser's leathery hides as they promise a broadened calendar of events in the future.

Lesbian Festival
December, Various locations
www.lesbianfestival.nl

2004 saw the first ever Amsterdam Lesbian Festival and already the girls showed up the boy with a genuine week-long festival that wasn't just another dance party but also had forum workshops, films, performances, exhibitions and debates. For one reason or another 2006 event was cancelled, and since then its been pretty quiet on the dyke front. Keep an eye ou for flyers or check www.amsterdam4gays.com to see if another event is in the making.

World AIDS Day
December 1, Various locations

A week-long **Take Care -Living PositHIV** awareness campaign by **Schorer**, the **AIDS Fond** and various gay businesses culminates in the **Lovedance** party at Paradiso.

Roze Filmdagen
December, Filmhuis Cavia, Cinema de Balie & Filmmuseum
www.rozefilmdagen.nl

The 'Pink Film Days' Gay & Lesbian film festival screens international and local queer-theme films and videos, discussions and forums. Meanwhile check www.amsterdam4gays.com fo the **'Gay Classic Movie Night'**, first wednesday of every month at 8.30pm in Pathe de Mur cinema, Vijzelstraat 15, or ask at **Pink Point**.

Skinhead Weekends
Various events throughout the year
www.agskins.nl

The only gay skins group remaining in mainland Europe, these guys stage great shaved cropped events like fetish parties, get-togethers, dinners, booze-ups and the judging of **M Gay Skinhead Europe**. Orange weekend held every Queen's Day weekend, Summer weeken in July & Skinterklaus in December, as well as other events throughout the year. No Nazi c White Power bullshit.

AIDS Fonds
www.aidsfonds.nl

Since 1985 the National AIDS fundraising organisation.

AIDS/STD Line
0900 204 2040 (10c/min)

24 hour service for AIDS and STD information in Dutch and English.

Akantes
Not on Map
Nieuwe Herengracht 95
+31 20 625 2066
Wednesday and Thursday
Noon – 5pm
www.akantes.nl

Formerly known as the **Women's House** and focusing only on women's emancipation, this organisation changed names and now focusses on emancipation for everyone, providing internet courses, a free internet café and a library of women's novels.

COC
Map 63, p.24
Rozenstraat 14
+31 20 626 3087 (office hours)
www.cocamsterdam.nl

The national lesbian and gay emancipation organisation, COC was instrumental in the legalisation of homosexuality in 1971. The COC has offices, meeting rooms and holds social occasions in virtually every major city across Holland. Unfortunatley the Amsterdam chapter of the COC closed its doors due to financial problems in 2006 and this once vibrant centre of queer life has become a ghost house, with only a few offices open and the occasional meeting taking place there. There are plans to re-open the building soon, but when is anyone's guess.

GALA
(Gay And Lesbian Amsterdam)
Not on Map
+31 20 676 2317
www.gala-amsterdam.nl

With their focus on highlighting Gay & Lesbian visibility, if there's a funky gay street party happening in Amsterdam chances are non-profit group GALA are involved. Instrumental in the popular open air parties on the **Homomonument** for **Queen's Day, Liberation Day** & **Amsterdam Pride's Summercamp**, they also stage the **SOS** Safe Sex parties at the **Eagle** and are a driving force behind the charity **World AIDS Day** event; the fabulous **Lovedance**.

GG&GD
Not on Map
Sexually Transmitted Diseases Clinic
Nieuwe Achtergracht
+31 20 555 5370
STD examinations: Mon - Fri
8:30-10:30am & 1:30 - 3:30pm
www.ggd.amsterdam.nl

Over a decade ago, for my first ever HIV test with my first ever boyfriend we waited in a sterile Melbourne hospital for our blood to be taken. Ken was a nurse and so terrified a colleague might see us he began to tap dance in the corridor to calm his nerves (Gay men, go figure!). So, God forbid you should ever have the ignomy of having a STD or HIV test done in Amsterdam. Not only can't you make an appointment, but you must arrive at the crack of dawn to take a number and wait in a line sometimes so long it's been known to snake out the door. Still, once you DO get to see a professional in a white coat they do try to make your time as quick and painless as is humanly possible.

Gay & Lesbian Switchboard

+31 20 623 6565
Daily noon – 10pm
Saturday/Sunday 4pm - 8pm
www.switchboard.nl
www.homoseks.nl

The Gay and Lesbian Switchboard is a fantastic resource, answering all types of questions about gay and lesbian Holland; from where to go dancing to health & relationship issues (although they won't be able to tell you if your bum *does* look big in that). Friendly and extremely helpful. Their website has an extensive links page.

HIV Vereniging (HIV Foundation)

Map 79, p.35
Eerste Helmersstraat 17
+31 20 616 0160
www.hivnet.org

Contact group and help line for people living with HIV/AIDS. Weekly Friday clinics 7pm till 9pm on-the-spot HIV tests with results in 15 minutes. Due to demand, appointments must be made between 2pm and 6pm. Cost €15. Also free Hepatitis B vaccinations. **HIV Café Tuesday evenings and Wednesday lunchtimes.**

International Homo/ Lesbian Information centre & Archives

Not on Map
Oosterdokseiland
+31 20 606 0712
www.ihlia.nl

IHLIA combines the **Homodok** and **Lesbian Archives** creating the largest gay, lesbian, bisexual, transgender & queer library collection in the Netherlands. In 2007 they move to the enormous new ten story public library (Openbare Bibliotheek Amsterdam) next to Centraal Station, as a special collection housed in the new library, with its own info counter and staff.

Meldpunt Vrouwenopvang

+31 20 611 6022
www.vrouwenopvang-ams.nl

Help line for women dealing with violent relationships.

Pink Point

Map 58, p.26
@ Homomonument
Westermarkt
(corner Keizersgracht and Raadhuisstraat)
+31 20 428 1070
Open daily 10am – 6pm
Limited opening hours in the dead of winter
www.pinkpoint.org

A friendly face, free advice and healthy amounts of good humour are just three of the services provided by the volunteers at Pink Point – the gay and lesbian information kiosk next to the **Homomonument**. Need to know the hottest club, best place for shopping or the cruisiest sauna (or, the cruisiest shopping, hottest sauna and best club) then swing by our all weather kiosk on the Westermarkt. Originally run from an old ice-cream cart temporarily set up for the Amsterdam Gay Games in 1998, Pink Point has now become the world's only 7-day-a-week gay & lesbian information kiosk. Pink Point's very presence as Amsterdam's official, openly gay tourist information center speaks volumes about the city's famed tolerance and image as a Gay Capital of Europe. Of course, all sexual bents are welcome here.

Schorer

Not on Map
Sarphatistraat 35
+31 20 573 9444 (Schorer Gay & Lesbian Health)
www.schorer.nl

Specialising in health and welfare issues for gays, lesbians, transgender & bisexuals Schorer (in conjunction with the G&L Switchboard) dispenses info about HIV/AIDS, STDs & other health issues. It also organises counselling services & a 'buddy' program for people with HIV/AIDS. Website only in Dutch.

YOUR WEEKLY CULTURAL GUIDE.

The Homomonument

Homomonument

Map B, p.24
@ Westermarkt
(Corner Keizersgracht and
Raadhuisstraat)
www.homomonument.com

Between 1933 - 1945 an estimated 100,000 German men were arrested as homosexuals, 50,000 officially sentenced and, during World War II, up to 15,000 were sent to Nazi concentration camps. Heinrich Himmler, a key architect in the Nazi killing machine, described their fate:

"These people will obviously be publicly degraded ... and handed over to the court. After, they will be taken to concentration camps and...they will be shot..." It's believed up to 60% of these men died. Despite such atrocities, German law criminalising homosexuality wasn't abolished until 1969.

Yet, just five short years after the end of the horrors of World War II, the fledgling gay rights organisation COC had, as the feature cover of its magazine *'Vriendschap'* (Friendship), a dedication to the deceased *"stigmatised and murdered in Nazi concentration camps during 1940 – 1945"*. Niek Engelschman – one of the founders and first chair of the COC, and whose name now adorns the bridge overlooking the Homomonument – declared: *"Has anyone ever had the moral courage to publicly commemorate our deceased brothers?"*

On May 4th 1970, two members of an Amsterdam homosexual youth group (AJAH) were arrested for disturbing the peace. Their only crime was the 'improper' laying of a wreath that interrupted the National Remembrance ceremony on Dam Square. The following day – ironically Liberation Day – fourteen AJAH members were arrested for handing out information detailing the persecution of homosexuals.

The ensuing public debate, with questions even being put to the Prime Minister, eventually led – through numerous committees and work groups over a period of 17 years - to the establishment of the world's first monument to the persecution of gays and lesbians: the Homomonument.

At the bend in the canal wall of the Keizersgracht, local artist Karin Daan designed a triangular 'jetty' out of pink granite - the pink triangle being the sign homosexual men were forced to wear in Nazi concentration camps. In addition, her unique design extended onto the Westermarkt, positioning a 60cm high triangular podium to the left and a memorial triangle embedded into the cobblestones to the right of the Westerkerk (the protestant 'West Church'). Each triangle measures 10 x 10 x 10 meters, connected by a line of pink granite stones to create one large triangle with sides of 36 meters. Although monumental in scale, her design is an elegant solution that not only situates a memorial to the persecution of homosexuals into the streetscape but also embeds into the very fabric and psyche of the city a powerful metaphor of the largely unseen presence of gay men and lesbians.

Each element of the Homomonument relates to the city of Amsterdam not only in a physical manner but also in a metaphorical sense. Embedded into the cobblestones the 'memorial triangle' contains a line of poetry by the renowned Dutch gay poet Jacob Israel de Haan (1881 – 1924): *"Such an endless desire for friendship"* (*"naar vriendschap zulk een mateloos verlangen"*).

This triangle – pointing coincidentally to the nearby Anne Frank House, the centre for the struggle against fascism, anti-Semitism and racism - has come to represent the past and historical persecution.

The tiered triangle leading down into the water of the Keizersgracht, points to the National War Memorial on Dam Square. It represents the present and inspires all who come to lay flowers, or who sit in quiet contemplation, to be eternally vigilant, lest the waters of intolerance ever rise again.

The raised 'podium triangle' – pointing to the nearby COC, the centre for the struggle for lesbian and gay liberation in the Netherlands – was intended by Daan to become a platform for performances, a 'soapbox' to express views and a "jumping off point" into the future.

On September 5th 1987, exactly 100 months after the first initiative, the Homomonument was declared open to the public. Annually, the focus for commemoration of World War II on 4th May, it's also the location for gay and lesbian parties on Koninginnedag (the Queen's birthday on 30th April), Liberation Day (5th May) and in August, Amsterdam's Gay Pride celebrations.

In 2003 a well-needed 'face-lift' replaced the original worn surface with thicker, more durable granite and completed Karin Daan's original design of a truly stepped platform floating above the Keizersgracht's murky depths.

In 2007 The Homomonument Foundation was set up to further the aims of the Homomonument; as a national memorial for homosexuals who were persecuted in the Second World War; a living monument as a source of inspiration for LGBT people today; and a call for vigilance against present and future oppression of LGBT people worldwide.

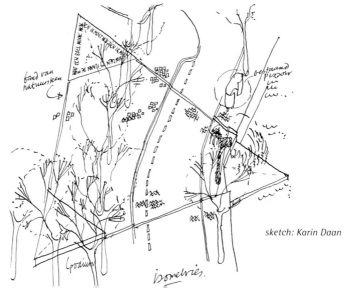

sketch: Karin Daan

Acupuncture

Leon d'Oliveira
Not on Map
Krügerplein 21 hs
+31 20 4180 410
http://www.acupunctuur-japans.nl/

Truly, the only time you're likely to leave satisfied after experiencing a little prick.

Masseur

Detlef Wittgens
Not on Map
Lijnbaansgracht 263
+31 20 4216 189/0653453081

Along with normal relaxation, pain relief & hot stone massages Detlef has the ultimate indulgence: chocolate massages. Apparently cacao contains the same stuff we produce when we're in love & has numerous anti-aging benefits for the skin - and all this time I've just been eating it!

Therapy/Life Coaching

Dr Daan Goedhart
Not on Map
Wittenburgergracht 10
+31 20 627 2813
www.ret-coach-daan.uwnet.nl

Solving stress & offering assistance toward better self confidence & more positive lives. Everyone should have a therapist called Dr Good Heart!

Fenomeen Sauna

Not on Map
Eerste Schinkelstraat 14
+31 20 671 6780
Women Only: Mon 1pm-11pm
Mixed Tues - Sun
Entry: €7 before 5pm,
€8 after 5pm.
www.saunafenomeen.nl

Women Only on Monday this sauna attracts a significant number of lesbians enjoying the unique 'alternative' surroundings & its organic juices & herbal teas. Mixed use all other days.

Fix

Not on Map
Laurierstraat 74-3
+31 (0) 6 1976 6726
www.fixonline.nl

Wolter (a Pink Point volunteer and one of our cute cover boys) gives fantastically relaxing and rejuvenating reiki and craniosacral therapy sessions that will help you balance body, mind & spirit. A perfect antidote for that jet lag!

Het Marnix

Not on Map
Marnixplein 1
+31 20 524 6000
www.hetmarnix.nl
Nude swimming Tue 9 - 10pm

The recently renovated Marnix, with 25 meter pool, sauna, spa, health club and the chic **ZinK** café, always draws a lot of gays and lesbians. Home pool of gay swim team Upstream, it also hosts nude swimming once a week, where about 50 gay men (with the occassional dyke and lost straight boy) lounge around in the water listening to classical music and chatting. Although most come for the 'back-to-nature' feeling, there's a little bit of underwater stroke practice in the corners.

Netzo Gay Volleyball
Not on Map
Sporthal Zeeburg
Insulindeweg 1001
Fridays 7–9pm & 9–11pm
www.netzo-amsterdam.nl

Established in 1998 they now have 90 members - evenly divided into mens & womens teams of various levels who compete both nationally and internationally.

Rainbow Squash
Not on Map
Frans Otten Stadion
IJsbaanpad 43
www.rainbowsquash.com

Rainbow Squash Amsterdam is (not surprisingly) a squash club for gays & lesbians. Main club activity is Friday evening from 7pm until 9.30pm where men & women (beginners & advanced) get together to belt a few balls around. First time is free, with yearly membership costing €120. They also organise the annual **Gay Pride** Squash Tournament, with participants from many countries.

Smashing Pink
Not on Map
www.smashing-pink.nl

Fond of bashing a few furry balls around, then join (self proclaimed) Europe's first ever Gay & Lesbian tennis club for a gay ol game of hit and giggle (actually, their 350 members take it quite seriously competing nationally & internationally).

Splash Health Club
Map 64, p.24
Looiersgracht 26-30
Lijnbaansgracht 241
+31 20 624 8404
Open 7 days 7am to 12pm
www.splashhealthclubs.nl

If you're one of those types that sweats when you're chatting someone up then this is the place for you. Not strictly gay & lesbian it is however, incredibly popular amongst inner-city queer gym rats (and quite a few flabbier types that just go to ogle the action in & out of the showers, change rooms, saunas, etc). A few years back Splash opened a second more 'kids friendly' (ie: creche facilities) gym on Lijnbaansgracht behind Leidseplein. You'd think it would attract more straights but this place is just wall-to-wall gay.

Tijgertje
Not on Map
+31 20 673 2458
www.tijgertje.nl

Gay & Lesbian sport club that organises badminton, basketball, Bodyshape, Condition training, HIV swimming, Karate, Special needs swimming, Tij-Bo, Volleyball, Wrestling, Yoga & Self-defence classes.

Upstream Amsterdam
Not on Map
for full details check
www.upstreamamsterdam.nl

Established in 1996 Upstream has over 100 swimmers, from beginners to advanced - and they even a synchronised swim team (how very Gay!). They mainly train in the newly renovated **Marnix** sports complex four times a week.

Zuiderbad
Map 84a, p.35
Hobbemastraat 26
(near Rijksmuseum)
Nude swimming Sunday 4.30 - 5.30pm

One of the country's oldest & most beautiful swimming pools, the Zuiderbad was built originally in 1912 as a centre for locals to learn how to ride bicycles. The nude swimming sessions here are a little less cruisy than in the Marnix pool.

PRESS & PUBLICATIONS

Amsterdam Gay Map
Various venues

For those having to squint at our maps, the regular version of the Amsterdam Gay Map is available free from **Pink Point**, and most Gay & Lesbian venues.

Amsterdam Weekly
Various locations
www.amsterdamweekly.nl

This great free English language paper is not much more than 3 years old, yet it has managed to win a bundle of European newspaper awards. Articles written by locals will give you a feel for what's happening in town and they have extensive music, stage, art, film, club, and (gay and lesbian) event listings.

Butt
Various bookshops
www.buttmagazine.com

Remember those cheap nasty gay mags with grainy black & white pics of ordinary blokes baring their arses you used to read one handed as a teenager? Well, this funky lil' magazine put together in an Amsterdam basement is for you. Of course, we only buy it for the cheeky articles!

Fantastic Man
Various bookshops
www.fantasticmanmagazine. com

Gentlemen's style journal from the creators of Butt, with fashion photos and interviews, in English.

Gay Krant
Various bookshops
www.gaykrant.nl

This glossy magazine is a Dutch institution and was instrumental in successfully campaigning for gay marriage a few years ago. Published every 2 weeks in Dutch only. Mainly for men.

Gay News
Various locations
www.gay-news.com

The largest gay monthly publication in Holland provides news, gossip, clubbing information, reviews & feature articles (mainly for men). Most articles are in Dutch & English. Available in bookshops for just under €4 or free in selected gay venues 2 weeks after publication.

Gay & Night
Various locations
www.gay-night.nl

Monthly magazine, most articles in Dutch & English. Mainly for men. Available at bookshops for €3.60 or free in selected gay venues 2 weeks after publication.

GLU (Girls Like Us)
Various bookshops
www.glumagazine.com

The sister version of Butt, GLU (girls like us) was created as an antidote to the vanilla representation of lesbians. Just as funky as their bum chum brothers, this cool little mag is made in Amsterdam and published in New York.

Het Parool
Newsagents
www.parool.nl

Amsterdam's daily Dutch newspaper has a great Saturday Arts supplement PS with an extensive agenda of Gay & Lesbian events in town.

Winq
Various bookshops
www.winqmagazine.com

Dutch language men's glossy fashion & features magazine published every 2 months.

Zij aan Zij
Newsagents
www.zijaanzij.nl

Dutch language women's kinda' glossy magazine published every 6 weeks.

TELEVISION

MVS TV
Saturday 8pm - 9pm
SALTO A1
www.mvs.nl

Every Saturday evening local Amsterdam station SALTO A1 broadcasts gay & lesbian programs (mostly in Dutch).

RADIO

MVS Radio
Mon to Sat: 7pm- 8pm
Sundays: 6pm - 8pm
FM 106.8
www.mvs.nl

MVS also produces 14 hours per week of gay & lesbian related radio programming on 106.8 FM. In Dutch. Tune in to the Disco Dimension every first and third Saturday night.

INTERNET

Amsterdam4gays
www.amsterdam4gays.com

The City-sanctioned official gay portal (you'll meet a few non-official gay portals in the darkrooms) for Amsterdam has always up-to-date info on parties, special events and a tourist guide. Produced by the boys from Nighttours (see below) we recommend you check it out for its up-to-date agenda before trekking out to some obscure party in some god forsaken venue just to discover it had been cancelled the week before.

Night Tours
www.nighttours.nl

A great online 'virtual tour' of the Amsterdam Gay boy (and girl) scene built by 2 local lads including their accurate agenda & pics of parties in Amsterdam as well as a growing number of international cities.

Gay Amsterdam
www.gayamsterdam.com

Online 'sister' of monthly glossy **Gay News** magazine, with subscriber porn galleries, contact classifieds, news & accommodation lisitings. In Dutch & English.

Gay Amsterdam Links
www.gayamsterdamlinks.com

Extensive listing of virtually every Amsterdam-based gay website; including restaurants, accommodation, gay portals (you've probably met a few of them downstairs at **The Eagle**!), search engines, health & general info. Text in Dutch but subject headings (mostly) English.

Gay Go
www.gaygo.nl

A great online resource for (almost) all your party needs: order tickets online for parties in Amsterdam, Rotterdam, Cologne, Brussels & more (often much cheaper than at the club door). Also organises bus trips to most of the major dance events & pics of previous gigs.

I Amsterdam
www.iamsterdam.com

The City of Amsterdam's official English-language website chock full of handy info about living, working & having fun in town, as well as extensive Gay & Lesbian info.

Lesbisch Pagina
http://lesbisch.pagina.nl

Dutch language portal of Lesbian (and some Gay) links.

Amsterdam Gay Guided City Walk

gayguidedtours@gmail.com
Sms or call +31 (0) 6 4493 6483

Take a private walking tour of Amsterdam. Depending on what you want you can make a tour through the historical medieval centre, the luxury canal belt and the Jordaan or a gay tour in which you'll pass by the main cruising places of the last 400 years. Approximately 2 hours. Call Freek for more info.

Canal Bus

+31 20 623 9886
www.canal.nl

A great way to see Amsterdam, with hop on and off day tickets available from kiosks around town, including Centraal Station, Leidseplein and Pink Point. Three different routes, with 14 stops passing all the main tourist attractions, plus discount vouchers for various attractions are included in one ticket. An easy and fun way to see the city, without having to worry about being bowled over by one of the thousands of Amsterdam bikes.

Mac Bike Gay Tour

Not on Map
Weteringschans 2,
Mr. Visserplein 2 or
Marnixstraat 220
+31 20 620 0985
www.macbike.nl

If you're on a tighter budget or just not into the group thing, you might want take this DIY tour of the gay scene. For €1.50 pick up this brochure at Pink Point or get it free if you rent your bike at Mac Bike. Follow the two gay tours - one historical (includes the Homomonument, Rembrandtplein and Vondel Park) and one hysterical (a tour of gay bars and clubs).

Orange Bike Rental & Tours

Not on Map
Singel 233
+31 20 528 9990
www.orangebike.nl

This new bike rental and tour company offers historical, architectural, culinary, beach and gay tours. For €27 (including one drink) the three and a half hour gay tour highlights all the main gay attractions in the city starting at the Schreierstoren in the east part of town, going through all the main gay areas, the Homomonument, and the red light district. A very comprehensive and detailed look at all aspects of gay life in Amsterdam, from political, historical and cultural viewpoints.

Index

About the author:

If, 20-odd years ago, anyone had asked the gangly Australian farm boy what his dream was, he may well have wistfully sighed: "To be married to the man on the packs of Chesty Bonds underwear, living in Amsterdam and working as a writer, with the occasional torch song routine at some smoky gin joint." Darren Reynoldson is just such a wanker.

Formerly a writer and director of Australian Government propaganda videos, Darren threw his lucrative career in style over substance away, to live in Amsterdam and write his great unfinished novel. Unfortunately, going out drinking and staying up late a LOT achieved only the opinionated piece of fluff you're now holding.

Now enslaved as a copywriter for a local internet advertising agency, Darren also subjects cyber-tourists to his (somewhat more sanitised) Homo & Metrosexual reviews as an I-Ambassador for the City of Amsterdam's portal www.iamsterdam.nl.

In a ceremony in Amsterdam, April 2001, Darren and his partner Thomas became Australia's first legally married gay couple. He's still thinking about the possibility of contemplating starting his novel, the torch song routine and learning to accept that the only six pack he'll possess will have a Heineken logo on it somewhere.

All comments, updates, suggestions and streams of abuse can be directed to getbent@pinkpoint.org where Darren will gladly thank you or advise you to upgrade your sense of humour.